Newcastle
City Council

Newcastle Libraries and Information Service

☎ **0845 002 0336**

Due for return	Due for return	Due for return
– 7 OCT 2010		

Please return this item to any of Newcastle's Libraries by the last
date shown above. If not requested by another customer the loan
can be renewed, you can do this by phone, post or in person.
Charges may be made for late returns.

ROUTEMASTER
Retrospective

THE ORIGINAL LONDON TRANSPORT SIGHTSEEING TOUR

Catch this Bus from:
VICTORIA STATION
MARBLE ARCH (SPEAKERS CORNER)

The Original LONDON TRANSPORT SIGHTSEEING TOUR

Catch this Bus from:
PICCADILLY CIRCUS (HAYMARKET)
BAKER STREET STATION

LONDON TRANSPORT

WLT762

Matthew Wharmby
and Geoff Rixon

Ian Allan PUBLISHING

Front cover: The drastic changes to London's bus services implemented during the 1980s drove crew operation and the Routemaster out of the suburbs. Introduced on 16 June 1973 as a localisation of the Manor House-Stratford end of the 241, route 230 would lose its conductors on 31 January 1981. At the time of this May 1976 shot RM587 (WLT 587) was allocated to Leyton, and with St Saviour's Anglican Church as a picturesque backdrop, is seen heading south down Markhouse Road towards Stratford. Like the majority of RMs withdrawn during the purge of conductors during the period covered by this book RM587 was scrapped, its final garage being Elmers End, from where it was withdrawn in August 1985. *Steve Smith collection*

Back cover (top): The 149, at its heart a long slog up and down the arrow-straight Hertford Road before crossing the river twice through the City of London, was a direct replacement for trolleybus route 649. It operated Routemasters in three distinct spells — firstly from its inception on 19 July 1961 until its RMs gave way to DMs in 1974, then with the splendid RCLs from 1980 to 1984, and again with RMs until OPO conversion on 7 February 1987. In this 27 March 1982 view at Lower Edmonton RM232 (VLT 232) is fresh out of overhaul and allocated to Edmonton garage. It would be withdrawn from Tottenham in January 1991 and exported to Norway. The 149, although pulled back in 1984 from Victoria to Waterloo and then in 1999 to Liverpool Street, was subsequently projected through to London Bridge, although its northern terminus was curtailed at Edmonton Green in 2004. It is now a 'bendy-bus' route. *Geoff Rixon*

Back cover (middle): The 37 seemed to be a bastion of stability in a world of bewildering change. Converted from RTL to RM in December 1962, it was RML-operated for 20 years, only going over to OPO on 21 June 1986. For its last decade of crew operation the 37's three operating garages' RMLs were the only long-wheelbase Routemasters allocated there specifically for the 37, and RML2610 (NML 610E), seen motoring peacefully along Sheen Road towards Richmond on 15 August 1981, was a Hounslow bus. After its withdrawal with the 15 in August 2003, this was another Routemaster to find its way to Norway. *Geoff Rixon*

Back cover (bottom): In its heyday the 65 was a long route linking Chessington Zoo and Ealing Broadway, but it operated RMs only between 19 October 1975 and 1 February 1986, when OPO Metrobuses took over. For a spell Kingston and Norbiton garages shared the honours, in a split roster that became useful when subsidence rendered Petersham Road in Ham impassable for some weeks on two occasions in 1979. At Surbiton in the first week of September 1982 we see Kingston's RM983 (WLT 983) leading Norbiton-based RM401 (WLT 401), the latter turning short. RM983 would be withdrawn from Victoria in May 1986 and scrapped three years later, while RM401 would perish in March 1985, Norbiton being its final garage. The 65, though subsequently split in two and curtailed from the north at Kingston since 1987, continues to be the principal route into Kingston. *Geoff Rixon*

Previous page: Not every change in the 1980s meant gloom and doom for the Routemaster — even in the years of mass withdrawals those in power recognised the role the RM family had still to play in London. The transformation of the mundane Round London Sightseeing Tour into the *Original* London Sightseeing Tour on 22 February 1986 was a stroke of genius; the replacement of 12 Metrobuses with 50 Routemasters, many of which were converted to open-top like RM762 (WLT 762), revitalised the London tour market at a stroke. Routemaster operation on London tour duties lasted for over a decade, but RM762 was withdrawn earlier, in 1993, and scrapped. *Geoff Rixon*

Contents

First published 2007

ISBN (10) 0 7110 3155 X

ISBN (13) 978 0 7110 3155 5

Published by Ian Allan Publishing

an imprint of Ian Allan Publishing Ltd, Hersham, Surrey KT12 4RG

Printed in England by Ian Allan Printing Ltd, Hersham, Surrey KT12 4RG

Code: 0704/B3

Visit the Ian Allan Publishing website at www.ianallanpublishing.com

Foreword

THE Routemaster is gone. Other than two vestigial Heritage services to serve as a reminder of happier times, the Routemaster took with it the London Transport legacy of a unified fleet with high-quality standardised buses. In latter days the Routemaster, in itself merely the final development of the traditional open-backed, front-engined London bus, would transmute from demonstrating not only London Transport's continuity of economically sound designs built to accentuate their surroundings to become an irreplaceable symbol of the capital itself. Without it a good deal of London's unique soul has been taken away.

This book covers, route by route, the commencement of the withdrawal of the Routemaster fleet, a process that between 1982 and 1989 accelerated to drive crew operation out of London's suburbs. The casual observer of the 1980s would discern little amiss from the large numbers of crew-operated buses — all owned and run by the one London Transport — still operating blithely in outer London. But so much would change, so quickly, and this book is intended as a snapshot of a *status quo* that, at the time, had seemed so invulnerable.

In the 1990s, having survived mass withdrawals arising from OPO conversions and endured the division and privatisation of London Buses, the Routemaster was still in there, hanging on — and as its reward for enduring such privation was treated to a new lease of life reflecting its cultural importance and continuing popularity with passengers. That refurbishment programme secured the remaining vehicles the decade of continued service that has only just ended, three months short of an unassailable 50 years.

Matthew Wharmby
Walton-on-Thames
January 2007

Above: The constant changes of national and local government in the period covered by this book gave rise to several changes of mind as the Routemaster family was first revitalised, then condemned, then reprieved again. In 1980 the need for the buses was so great that even the coach versions, the sublime RCLs, were bought back from London Country and pressed into use as buses. RCL2249 (CUV 249C), allocated to Stamford Hill for the 149 in August 1980, is captured during an early foray to the 253, the garage's major route then and today. Four years later it was withdrawn and sold to PVS for scrap. *Geoff Rixon*

Introduction

HAD its successors done the job asked of them, the Routemaster would have had a much shorter length of service than that which it ultimately enjoyed. Until the privilege of specifying and building its own buses was taken away from London Transport, its bus types would serve their 20 years without incident and then be replaced seamlessly by vehicles of equal or superior specification — more seats, more powerful engines, better blinds and so on. Out of this process of continuous development was born the Routemaster. But with the Merlins, Swifts and Fleetlines that era of improvement seemed to stop. The personal service afforded by a change-giving, helpful conductor was replaced by unco-operative fare-collection machinery, while comfortable seating gave way to crush-loading standing and the certainty of long trunk routes degenerated into frustrating short hops fighting London's increasingly stifling traffic.

To be fair, socio-economic changes, particularly the explosion in car ownership, were making bus operation in the capital very difficult by the late 1960s. London Transport believed that its solution, the Reshaping Plan of 1966, would slow the rot of falling ridership and spiralling running costs. It did neither, creating new problems of its own as the off-the-shelf vehicles purchased — untried, in enormous numbers — failed to perform to the standards of their predecessors and did not fit into the established system of overhaul and maintenance.

The Reshaping Plan envisaged crew operation eliminated entirely by 1978 and London's streets filled with single-deck standee buses operating a flat-fare system of shortened routes. The reality of 1978 was quite different — the majority of the Merlins and Swifts had been withdrawn after just five years, the double-deck solution in the form of the DMS was falling rapidly by the wayside, the Routemaster fleet was virtually intact, and at the start of the year there were even 200 RTs still in service. Clearly the Routemaster had regained the ascendancy and would be continuing as the backbone of the LT fleet until a purpose-built solution was developed — as might have been the case in 1967, had not the rear-engined FRM been denied production.

What might have been. Despite its popularity with drivers and engineers FRM1 (KGY 4D), the only rear-engined Routemaster, found itself shunted off to the far corners of the system on routes where just a single bus was required. Service at Croydon on the 233 was followed by a spell at Potters Bar on the 284, which was cut short following an accident with London Country Leyland National SNB92. In 1978 it was transferred to the Round London Sightseeing Tour, operated at the time by Stockwell garage, and is captured at Parliament Square in June 1980 wearing traditional London Transport livery. In 1982 it was retired to become part of the London Transport Museum display stock. Lately it has seen more use, stealing the spotlight on the last day of crew operation on the 73, 3 September 2004, and more recently as a guest on the Heritage sections of the 9 and 15 on 17 September 2006. Geoff Rixon

Above: The time-honoured underlined <u>LONDON TRANSPOR</u>T fleetname in gold leaf was one of the many items of Routemaster presentation to bite the dust during the lead-up to this account. First to go was the underlining, producing a rather plain effect before a revised livery appeared in 1974, featuring a white band, solid white roundel and plain white fleetnumbers. Representing the interim situation is Streatham's RM1376 (376 CLT), seen passing Brixton garage on 17 August 1981. It remained based at Streatham until December 1983 and was sold for scrap six months later, unusually being broken up in Wales. *Geoff Rixon*

Right: As the Merlin, Swift and Fleetline families of the 1970s began to disgrace themselves to an extent that alarmed London Transport, the general reliability of the Routemaster became all the more important, holding together as it did a troubled organisation in an equally fraught decade. One most unusual expedient was the pressing into service of a handful of the former British European Airways front-entrance Routemasters; the route chosen was the 175, on which RMA4 (NMY 629E), allocated to North Street, is seen at Romford station in March 1976. Only a vestigial slipboard provides passengers with any clue as to where the bus is heading. When the spares shortage eased, the RMAs were redeployed as staff buses and trainers. RMA4 spent the 1980s in the latter role at West Ham and Upton Park, falling to the scrapman's torch in 1992. *Dave Brown*

Above: The renaissance of the Routemaster in the early 1980s was due largely to its sidelining at London Country, the former Country Area of London Transport. In the decade since the National Bus Company took over the green buses surrounding the capital, severe cost-cutting had led to the widespread introduction of one-person operation. Coaches became buses, and the state of them deteriorated rapidly. The last RMCs ran for London Country in March 1980, and the majority were purchased by London Transport. On 16 May 1980 RMC1484 (484 CLT) shows its new ownership in the form of an LT roundel applied to its NBC leaf-green livery. Its learner driver has been assigned the roads of Thames Ditton, some 10 miles to the west of the bus's then home garage of Streatham. After a decade's use as a trainer RMC1484 was scrapped in June 1992. *Geoff Rixon*

Below: It seemed that the 1980s would bring an end to crew operation in London, so quick and thorough were the OPO conversion programmes of that decade. Among the Routemasters displaced was RM1183 (183 CLT), which was withdrawn from Bow in July 1987 but was still carrying its tourist posters for the 25 when captured in Twickenham the following April, whilst being driven on trade plates from the old AEC site at Southall to an alternative storage site at Fulwell. Its interesting post-London career was typical of that enjoyed by many RMs and included spells with Southend Transport and London & Country before sale to Nostalgiabus. Unfortunately, like the majority of Routemasters, RM1183 is no more, this bus having perished in a fire on 31 December 1997. *Geoff Rixon*

Right: The ultimate destination of the majority of Routemasters since the withdrawals commenced has been the scrapyard. The names Goodwin, PVS, Wigley and Wombwell Diesels and have struck fear into the hearts of enthusiasts since 1982, the second of these Yorkshire-based firms having taken RM1633 (633 DYE) for despatching after its withdrawal from the 30 at Clapton in February 1987. The contractors discovered that the toughly-built Routemaster was considerably harder to dismantle than the more modern types, this bus being hollowed out and windowless but still structurally intact. It is important to remember that scrapping can prolong the life of other members of a class, with the parts going back to London Transport for reuse in other examples. *Geoff Rixon*

As it turned out, the second-generation Metrobus and Titan OPO double-deckers proved sufficiently reliable for LT to shelve development work on a possible Routemaster successor (the XRM programme) and by 1983 had replaced most of the DMSs. But it wasn't vehicle policy that began to threaten the Routemaster; instead, the buses of London became a pawn in a bitter political tug-of-war between County Hall and Whitehall, two locations separated physically only by the Thames but ideologically by an abyss.

Once in the hands of Ken Livingstone (from May 1981) the Greater London Council unveiled bold plans for the future direction of London Transport. Quite reasonably, it was felt by the GLC that fares should be reduced and simplified to attract passengers away from cars — a policy that culminated in the Fares Fair programme of 4 October 1981. Conservative-controlled Bromley Council, however, resented the supplementary levy imposed on the rates to pay for Fares Fair, citing the borough's lack of an Underground service as grounds for opposition. Even as Fares Fair allowed passenger ridership to increase for the first time in 30 years, Bromley Council took London Transport to court. It lost, but a subsequent appeal to the High Court was upheld, and Fares Fair was ruled illegal. Thereafter, things started to go horribly wrong for London's buses. Fares had to be doubled from 21 March 1982, and passenger numbers plummeted to the extent that, in a desperate attempt to make savings, 15% of the scheduled service had to be removed on one brutal day, 4 September 1982. It was that day that saw the first normal Routemaster withdrawals.

Emboldened, the Conservative Government put in train plans that would remove the GLC altogether and restructure public transport nationwide. The Transport Act 1985 had its own sweeping ideals, predicting that deregulation of bus services would wipe out the perceived lethargic practices of old and promote competition, thereby bringing down costs. While deregulation in London was postponed pending feasibility studies, its bus routes were to be put out to competitive tender, a process which from mid-1985 began to introduce numerous independent operators — of sharply varying quality — and steadily reduced the proportion of red buses. London's system of tendering endured a frequently painful first decade, during which the London Buses Ltd organisation formed from London Transport was split into 11 wholly owned subsidiaries that were sold late in 1994. Although plans to deregulate London would eventually be abandoned, the prestige of 'London Transport' had been brought low, and only the Routemaster survived to personify memories of prouder times.

Bibliography

Books
Routemaster Requiem, Matthew Wharmby and Geoff Rixon (Ian Allan Publishing, 2006)
Routemaster Jubilee, Geoff Rixon (Ian Allan Publishing, 2004)
Routemaster, Volume 1, Ken Blacker (Capital Transport Publishing, 1991)
Routemaster, Volume 2, Ken Blacker (Capital Transport Publishing, 1992)

Periodicals and annuals
'The London Bus Review' series, LOTS, 1973-1992
London Bus Magazine quarterly, LOTS, 1972-present
The London Bus, monthly, LOTS, 1964-present
Buses, *Buses Extra* and *Buses Focus*, Ian Allan Publishing

Websites
Ian's Bus Stop (http://freespace.virgin.net/ian.smith/buses/ index.htm) by Ian Smith
London Bus Routes (www.londonbuses.co.uk) by Ian Armstrong

ONE

Reshaping Retrenched

THE first order of business as 1980 opened was to continue the process of restoring RMs to Central London routes where DMs and MDs had failed so dismally, and the 36 group was chosen as the pilot. In order to release the Routemasters for this task three of their routes had to succumb to doored buses of their own, but in the case of the 62 and 87 from Barking garage, these were the considerably more personable Titans, the 62 being converted to crew T on 12 January, the 87 on the 26th. The third source was the 122 at Plumstead; this garage treated its incoming MD-class Scania/MCW Metropolitans rather better than Peckham had on the 36 group and liked them so much that it began to gather most of the class to use on its OPO routes as well.

The odd OPO conversion would still take place on a sporadic basis; on 27 September the 26 at Finchley became the first route to go over to OPO with M-class MCW Metrobuses. Saturday 27 September 1980 saw a sizeable programme centred on the Palmers Green–Enfield corridor, the 135 at Enfield being converted from RM to OPO DMS and the 298 and 298A, both formerly outer segments of the 29 and at this time both Palmers Green services, reconfigured; the 298 was one-manned with DMSs, while the 298A was withdrawn, its four buses seamlessly incorporated into a boost to the 121. In South East London Abbey Wood garage's 161A, the Petts Wood bifurcation of the 161, was withdrawn on 27 September, its buses joining the parent route.

Route 62
Converted from RM to crew T, 13 January 1980

So much for the brief fame that Barking's 1979 intake of RMs enjoyed through being the buses that displaced London Transport's last RTs on 7 April 1979; they lasted only nine months on the 62 before being displaced by the first crew-operated examples of the T-class Leyland Titan. RM1256 (256 CLT) is pictured on the final day of RT operation, having just taken over duty BK223, with the enthusiast crowds visible in the background outside Barking garage. It would pass to Peckham for the conversion back to RM of the 36 group and would be withdrawn from Westbourne Park in June 1989, ultimately being scrapped by PVS at Barnsley in June 1990. *Geoff Rixon*

Route 122
Converted from RM to crew MD, 3 February 1980

Right: A very long route with an allocation of 24 crew buses, the 122 was not to receive RMs until 22 April 1978, when the old Plumstead garage (AM) took on enough to replace its final RTs. One such new entrant was RM724 (WLT 724), seen at the Bexleyheath garage terminus of the time. The reversion of the 36 group to Routemaster operation at the start of 1980 was achieved by swapping those routes' Metropolitans for Plumstead's RMs. Crew Titans supplanted the 122's MDs at the start of 1983 and OPO followed on 23 April of that year. RM724 survived until July 1986, when it was removed from Wandsworth garage and dismantled to provide spare parts for Clydeside Scottish's growing fleet of Routemasters acquired to compete in the deregulated market. *Steve Smith collection*

Below: Woolwich market place is entirely deserted on 30 December 1979 as RM252 (VLT 252) passes through, stirring up that winter's slush. It was withdrawn from Merton in April 1985 and scrapped by PVS. *John Parkin*

Route 87
Converted from RM to crew T, 17 February 1980

Right: From seeing the generously provisioned route 87 and its 26 allocated RMs in 1980, the time-traveller would be surprised to see no sign of the route today; progressive swallowing-up, commencing with the replacement of the Rainham end by new route 287 in 1982, the Noak Hill end by the 374 in 1993 and the rump by the 5 in 2006, was yet to come. The 87 had been the penultimate RT route until 30 RMs arrived on 28 October 1978 to see off Barking's veterans, but these were to last little more than a year before crew Titans arrived at Barking to replace them. Transferred into Barking to see off the last RTs from the 62, RM408 (WLT 408), is seen working in Romford three months after that sad event. It was withdrawn from Camberwell in November 1985 but saw a new career with Kelvin Scottish. Subsequently owned by four preservationists in succession, it left these shores in 2005 for Sri Lanka, to assist displaced victims of the tsunami that struck on Boxing Day 2004. *Geoff Rixon*

Route 26
**Converted from RM to OPO M,
27 September 1980**

Left: The 26 was introduced on 13 January 1970 to fuse the Barnet end of the 260 with the Victoria end of the 2. Cricklewood and Finchley shared the honours, but the former's allocation was soon removed. The withdrawal of the 26 south of Golders Green from 28 October 1978 slashed its requirement from 15 buses to just four, rendering OPO distinctly more feasible. It was the first route to be one-manned with Metrobuses. On 10 February 1980 Finchley put RML2268 (CUV 268C) out in lieu of the usual RM, but this shot at the half-circle terminus at Golders Green doesn't show it making the best use of its extra eight seats. The 26 was withdrawn on 2 February 1991, most of its service being transferred to the back-roads minibus 326. RML2268 lasted till the one-manning of the 23 in November 2003 and was exported to Malaysia. *Geoff Rixon*

Route 135
**Converted from RM to OPO DMS,
27 September 1980**

Left: Longtime Enfield-area local route 135 came late to the Routemaster, finally gaining examples to replace its RTs on 16 January 1978. The Sunday service was already OPO with DMSs, and the weekday service would follow on 27 September 1980. The route vanished in the great programme of 4 September 1982, divided up between three other local services, but RM906 (WLT 906), seen plying its trade through Enfield Town in October 1979, would remain in service until withdrawn from Ash Grove in 1991. Two years of training duties followed before scrapping at PVS. *Geoff Rixon*

Route 161A
Withdrawn, 27 September 1980

Left: Having served Eltham and Mottingham on its way south from Woolwich, the 161 pair came to some confusion once Chislehurst was reached. Which way to go — turn left to Sidcup and Foots Cray, or keep going straight on to the quieter environs of Petts Wood? From 1950 a 161A was introduced to address traffic bound for the latter point, and on 21 May 1977 this was converted from RT to Routemaster, Abbey Wood garage fielding 13 RMs. On 27 September 1980 the need for two separate routes had dwindled to the extent that the 161A was incorporated into the 161 as a bifurcation. Ironically the suffix would reappear in 1991, the parent route having been diverted in a third direction from Chislehurst — west towards Bromley! Three days before the end of this particular 161A Abbey Wood's RM222 (VLT 222) reposes at Charlton. It was withdrawn from Edmonton in September 1985 and scrapped. *Steve Smith collection*

Route 298
Converted from RM to OPO DMS, 27 September 1980

Right: Journey's end for Routemasters on the 298 as Palmers Green's RM656 (WLT 656) brings down the curtain at the route's then Cockfosters terminus. One-manning did the 298 some good, doubling its peak vehicle requirement at the expense of the 298A (below), but this was the last day that Cockfosters would see RMs. This vehicle's last posting was to Bow, from where it was withdrawn in October 1984, sale to PVS following two months later.
Steve Smith collection

Route 298A
Withdrawn, 27 September 1980

Below: June 1980, and behind RM524 (WLT 524) Wood Green Shopping City is under construction atop the site of the old Noel Park & Wood Green station, closed in 1963 with the rest of the Palace Gates railway line. The 298A was introduced between Turnpike Lane and Oakwood on 7 September 1968, and its RTs were replaced by RMs on 24 January 1970. Operation was transferred from Palmers Green to Wood Green on 13 June of that year, a Saturday service being added on 16 January 1971. On 27 September 1980 the route was swallowed up by the extension of the 121 to Turnpike Lane. RM524 was withdrawn from Upton Park in February 1984 and scrapped by PVS in January 1985. *Dave Brown*

TWO

Fares Fair Foiled

SATURDAY 31 January 1981 saw substantial changes made to several routes. Most prominently the 55 at Leyton was restored to RM operation after eight years with DMSs, the 230 at the same garage being one-manned — but with Leyland Nationals (LSs). At Shepherd's Bush the 72 was converted from RM to DMS, while Plumstead's share of the 180 was converted from RM to crew MD. At night the N91 lost its RMs for crew Ms on 30 March, although from 25 April RMs were restored to routes N90, N92 and N93 in place of DMs.

On 25 April the 262, only RM again (ex-DM) since 14 October 1979 and the province of West Ham garage, was one-manned with DMSs. On the Wandsworth Road corridor the 168 was withdrawn altogether, this route another to have regained Routemasters from the DM class of crew-operated Fleetlines — but for little more than four months. Stockwell and Wandsworth moved the route's resources to the 170 on the same axis. Over in the City, Sunday-only 9A to Aldgate was withdrawn after only three months of operation, following a change of mind as to which roads in the Square Mile needed buses most on that day of the week. The last C-suffixed service, route 77C, was another weekend-only device and was withdrawn on

25 April (although the number would reappear on a school bus route 10 years later).

The Districts introduced on 1 October 1979 had created issues of their own regarding which types of vehicle were considered standard in each. The closure of Stonebridge and Middle Row garages on 15 August 1981 saw their services moved to brand-new Westbourne Park and vehicles redeployed to their 'correct' Districts — a process that saw Brixton's routes 109 and 133 regain RMs by taking them from the 33 and 281 at Fulwell, which lost its Routemasters entirely in favour of crew Metrobuses displaced from Stonebridge.

London Transport's bus conductors were undoubtedly some of the beneficiaries of the GLC's fares-reduction programmes of 1981. The first instalment, known as Fare Deal and implemented from 5 April, simplified the hitherto great variety of fares by introducing a flat fare of 25p in a new outer zone. Even before the brief flowering of Fares Fair, this was a step that would make it easier for OPO by taking much of the workload off the driver, who already had his or her work cut out in having to face increasing volumes of traffic. Then, from 4 October, Fares Fair reduced fares across the board by an average of 32% — an innovation that was not to last as its opponents took the matter to the courts.

Route 72
Converted from RM to OPO DMS, 31 January 1981

Left: Routemasters took over the 72 from Hammersmith garage on 14 December 1975, by which time the route was operating between East Acton and Tolworth Broadway, all services beyond that point to Esher, Hampton Court or Surbiton having been cut back. On 25 April 1975 RM2042 (ALM 42B) was captured at the East Acton (Brunel Road) terminus on a duty which would operate no further south than Kingston Vale, leaving the thrash along the Kingston by-pass to another 72. This bus was withdrawn from Norwood garage in April 1986 and scrapped by Trevor Wigley & Sons, of Carlton, South Yorkshire, in September 1989. *Colin Brown*

Above: Hammersmith Bridge presents a most handsome backdrop for Riverside's RM514 (WLT 514) on 3 September 1978 as it heads south. Between 1975 and 1982 and again between 1985 and 1991 the 72's Sunday service was extended from the Tolworth Broadway terminus of the time to reach Chessington Zoo. RM514 was an early casualty, coming off service at New Cross in September 1982 to be broken up by Vic Berry's employees at Aldenham seven months later, without even one last run north. *Steve Smith collection*

Left: The Shillibeer Routemaster allocated to Hammersmith garage, RM2184 (CUV 184C), was strictly limited to the 11, sneaking out on the 72 just once, on 27 January 1980, and this lucky shot was recorded as evening fell over Tolworth Broadway. By this time the splendid green and yellow livery commemorating the founder of London's horse buses was almost a memory, and this bus would go for repaint within days. Having gained a Leyland engine during its final overhaul, RM2184 would last until March 1987, when it was withdrawn from service at New Cross garage. It was despatched to PVS for scrapping three months later. *Geoff Rixon*

Route 230
Converted from RM to OPO LS, 31 January 1981

Right: Introduced on 16 June 1973 between Stratford and Manor House using five RMs from Leyton, the 230 allowed the 241 to fall back to Stratford and become a local service; all these roads were served by the 41 until traffic forced planners' hands. In 1976 RM587 (WLT 587) was one of Leyton's fleet, being seen in Markhouse Road during May of that year; it would be withdrawn from Elmers End in August 1985 and scrapped the same month. The 230 became more famous for converting to RT for a period during 1977 when Routemaster spares shortages were at a critical level, but OPO on 31 January 1981 saw LSs take over, due to the lack of OPO double-deckers at Leyton following the withdrawal of the 55's DMSs the same day. The 230 has since grown to become one of the most important routes in the area, now plying between Wood Green and Upper Walthamstow with an upper deck restored. *Steve Smith collection*

Route 9A
Withdrawn (again), 25 April 1981

Above: Two incarnations of route 9A ploughed a furrow over the 9 from Mortlake to Aldgate on Sundays only, deviating from the parent route by serving the Tower of London. The first, shared between Mortlake and Dalston, operated between 9 April 1971 and 28 October 1978 but was brought back on 31 January 1981, worked by the same two garages. A change of mind on the 9 road on 25 April of that year gave the Tower a through route instead in the shape of the 23, and the 9 has not operated east of the City since. During February 1981 Mortlake's RM1678 (678 DYE) passes through Hammersmith; upon closure of its home garage this bus would transfer to Stamford Brook, finishing there in June 1984 and succumbing to the scrapman three months later. *Geoff Rixon*

Route 77c
Withdrawn, 25 April 1981

Right: The complicated variations of the 77 service were identified by suffix letters according to which bridge they crossed on their way from South West London into the West End. The 77c's remit was weekends-only via Westminster Bridge, whilst the 77A ran via Lambeth Bridge and the 77 used Vauxhall Bridge. RMs converted Stockwell's Saturday-only allocation on 8 January 1972 and reached Merton's Sunday-only allocation on 15 December 1973. Having set off from King's Cross, Stockwell's RM986 (WLT 986) approaches Euston on Saturday 12 April 1980. The bus is fresh out of overhaul and only frontal advertising has yet been applied. That overhaul would be its last; once transferred to Kingston garage it became one of the first of the class to be withdrawn, in September 1982. Happily, further adventures beckoned in Canada. *Geoff Rixon*

Route 262
Converted from RM to OPO DMS, 25 April 1981

Above: Created to run between Leyton (Baker's Arms) and the Victoria & Albert Docks on New Year's Eve 1966 to replace the outer section of withdrawn East End fixture 26, route 262 was RML-operated from the start. On 7 September 1968 it was extended north to Chingford, gaining a West Ham allocation to join the existing Leyton workings, but on 16 June 1973 fell back to Walthamstow Central station, Leyton garage withdrawing other than at weekends. On the same date RMs replaced RMLs, while the Sunday workings had been OPO since 28 October 1972. The 262 was one of the routes selected for crew-operated Fleetlines, but the DM era lasted only from 22 April 1978 to 14 October 1979. The presence at Stratford of RML2718 (SMK 718F) on one of Leyton's Saturday workings on 14 July 1978 made it one of only four Routemasters possible on that day at that time, DMs being in charge on the rest of the 262. Having long outlasted not only all the Fleetlines but also the Titans that replaced them on the 262 not long after OPO conversion of the route, RML2718 survived all the way to 2005. Although one of Brixton's final RML complement, it was withdrawn some eight months before the end of regular Routemaster operation and exported to Japan. *Geoff Rixon*

Route 168
Withdrawn, 25 April 1981

Above: RMs displaced tram-replacement route 168's DMs from both Stockwell and Wandsworth garages on 15 December 1980, but the route was to be operated thus for only four months. The planners reasoned that the Wandsworth Road corridor into Westminster, Aldwych and points beyond was already served adequately by the 170 and withdrew the 168 on 25 April 1981. On the previous day Wandsworth-allocated RM1590 (590 CLT) makes the left turn from the Embankment into Northumberland Avenue — two roads now no longer served by London buses. This bus was treated to 1933-style livery to mark the London General subsidiary's unveiling in 1989, by which time it was allocated to Victoria. The closure of that garage saw it pass to Waterloo (RA), where it was withdrawn in April 1994. The most recently reported of three subsequent owners uses the vehicle as an IT trainer. *Steve Smith collection*

Left: Also marking the last day of the 168 route on 24 April 1981, RM40 (VLT 40) reposes at the Putney Heath stand. Following the withdrawal of the 168 (and projections here of the 28), this spot opposite the Green Man pub would continue to be used for peak-hour projections of the 77A from Wandsworth. At the time the stand formed a narrow through road to Putney Heath, but this was later filled in to create a turning-circle currently used by the 14. RM40 left the 168 for a new posting at Holloway and was sent for overhaul in mid-1982. Bow was to be its final garage, until May 1987, since when the bus has joined the ranks of preserved Routemasters and can regularly be seen at rallies. *Steve Smith collection*

Route 281
Converted from RM to crew M, 15 August 1981

Right: The exit of RMs from the 281 in favour of crew Ms was part of a complex three-way switch to restore the correct types into their respective Districts after the opening of a new garage upset the existing balance. The 281 had replaced trolleybus route 601 on 9 May 1962, using RMs from the beginning, and from 3 October 1965 expanded north of the 601's Twickenham terminus with a projection to Hounslow on Sundays in replacement of the 73, making it the major suburban carrier that it remains today. Comparatively little further alteration has been needed ever since, barring an extension a short way south of Tolworth to Chessington Industrial Estate between 1970 and 1987. A suburban route, the 281 was considered early for OPO, which was introduced on Sundays from 27 March 1971, but the rest of the route would not follow suit until 4 September 1982. On 15 July 1978 RM1152 (152 CLT) passes through Surbiton, once graced by the overhead wires once used by the 281's predecessor. *Geoff Rixon*

Right: RM2217 (CUV 217C), the last of the RM class built and later to gain eternal fame by being the last Routemaster scheduled for stage service, is seen in Surbiton on 14 August 1981, its last day allocated to Fulwell before moving to Brixton. On the following day Metrobus-operating Stonebridge garage, in Cardinal District, closed, operation of the 18 passing to brand-new Westbourne Park; the latter being an Abbey District garage, its drivers were not trained on Ms, so Stonebridge's Ms passed to Fulwell, displacing its RMs to Brixton for the 109 and 133, which released DMs to Westbourne Park. *Geoff Rixon*

Route 18A
Converted from RM to DM, 15 August 1981

Left: Introduced on 17 June 1967 to replace the 293, a peak-hour route running between Acton and Paddington, the 18A was so numbered to indicate an extension over the 18 route to King's Cross. This lasted only until 13 June 1970, but second thoughts brought it back as far as Baker Street from 28 October 1978. RM-operated by Middle Row from the start, its transfer to newly-opened Westbourne Park on 15 August 1981 obliged it to convert to DM, leaving Routemasters like RM838 (WLT 838) without employment. Seen on layover at Willesden Junction five days before the closure of Middle Row, this bus would continue to work until November 1994 — but a return to London saw it in service on the last day of Routemasters in normal service, 9 December 2005. The 18A, however, was withdrawn on 4 September 1982 without replacement. *Steve Smith collection*

THREE

The First Cut

THE overturning of Fares Fair by the Law Lords was not the kind of Christmas present most Londoners opened happily. After some years of overspending under the GLC, London Transport was informed that it had a statutory duty to break even, and accordingly fares had to double from 21 March 1982. Drastic savings now had to be made, and quickly. During the spring a considerable proportion of those sections of routes passing beyond the Greater London boundary were abandoned, and 4 September saw the implementation of the most extensive route-change programme since that which followed the strike of 1958.

During the summer of 1982 the 174 and 175 at North Street were turned over to crew T, with OPO to follow in 1983, and the 4 September scheme further laid the ground for future one-manning by converting the 83 (Alperton) and 105 (Southall) from RM to crew M and the 93 (Sutton) to DM. Routemaster-operated services withdrawn entirely were the 176A (latterly run by Walworth) and the long-established 94 (Catford and Bromley), though this latter route was split into two new services (208 and 261) that would be easier to convert to OPO when the time came.

OPO conversions on 4 September 1982 affected the 101 (Upton Park), 102 (Palmers Green), 104 (Holloway) and 196 (Stockwell) in their existing forms, though routes 187 (Alperton), 193 (Seven Kings) and 229 (Sidcup) were all shortened substantially. Most notably, the 106 was converted to OPO for a second time, although the Titans allocated to Ash Grove were a much better proposition than the DMSs of a decade earlier. At night two more routes succumbed in the shape of the N89 (Riverside) and N99 (West Ham), while conductors remained on Wandsworth's N68 and N88, though with DMSs rather than RMs.

As the year closed, crew Titans were replacing the RMs on the 58 out of West Ham, but already the first casualties had started to accrue to the Routemaster fleet. Between August 1982 and year's end more than 200 RMs were withdrawn, those with Simms electrics and/or Leyland engines being disposed of first.

Route 174
Converted from RM to crew T, summer 1982

RMs served nearly 16 years on the 174, a route that then, as now, plied between the Dagenham foundries and Noak Hill, north of Romford. North Street garage was in charge, with assistance from Hornchurch during the latter part of 1970, but from 29 March 1982 crew Titans started taking over, the inevitable OPO conversion being effected on 23 April 1983. RM688 (WLT 688) works through Romford Market on 15 September 1979. All that remains of this bus is its registration, which migrated to Volvo Olympian NV38 when its rightful owner was withdrawn in September 1996. *Geoff Rixon*

Route 175
Converted from RM to crew T, summer 1982

Right: The conversion of routes 174 and 175 at North Street from RM to crew T was carried out simultaneously, but the 175 had a grander history in the Romford area than the continuously local 174. Once shared by four garages, the 175 had been truncated considerably and was operated solely by North Street by 11 October 1975, when RTs were replaced by Routemasters; however, these, the first batch of former British European Airways RMAs, were not a success, and RTs returned the following September. Routemasters — this time RMs — came back on 19 March 1977, running between North Romford, Hillrise Estate and Dagenham, Ford Main Works. The irregular section north of the GLC border as far as Passingford Bridge survived the arrival of Titans from 29 March 1982 — but not by long, vanishing with the route's OPO conversion on 23 April 1983. North Street's RM1656 (656 DYE), seen in Romford on 15 September 1979, was sold to PVS in December 1993 after two years as a training bus following withdrawal from Norwood in July 1991. Its registration lives on, at present adorning a Wright-bodied DAF double-decker. *Geoff Rixon*

Route 94
Withdrawn, 4 September 1982

Left: For many years the major carrier into, through and out of South East London, the 94 was at its peak a lengthy and circuitous route that posed an operational problem in that it passed neither of its operating garages at Catford and Bromley. This situation was addressed on 4 September 1982 by splitting the route so that its separated portions did just that, the 208 running from Catford and 261 from Bromley. Having seen off South East London's last RTs on 27 August 1978, the replacement RMs would last less than four years on the 94 before the 208 and 261 took over, and these routes in turn would soon fall to OPO. Allocated to Catford and looking very smart indeed, RM1250 (250 CLT) is seen in April 1980, huddled around the back of Lewisham bus station with a DMS on the 70 tucked in behind. *Geoff Rixon*

Left: Another view of RM1250 (250 CLT) features it on 13 March 1982, passing beneath the pedestrian bridge that once separated the two halves of the Riverdale Centre in Lewisham. The bus was still allocated to Catford, where its remit included not merely the 94 but also the 1 and the 47, but in the intervening 3½ years had assumed partial Showbus status, with underlined LONDON TRANSPORT fleetname; pity that the radiator triangle has gone missing. Withdrawn from Peckham in June 1987, it enjoyed a brief spell with Stagecoach's Magicbus operation in Glasgow before succumbing to the scrapman's torch in the autumn of 1989. *Geoff Rixon*

Route 176A
Withdrawn, 4 September 1982

Right: Partner to the cross-town 176, route 176A commenced at Cannon Street (later Mansion House) and joined its parent at the Elephant, paralleling it all the way to Forest Hill. Its projections beyond this point to Catford or Lewisham had long since disappeared by the time RMs took over on 21 March 1976, the route by now being worked throughout by Walworth garage. With the decreasing viability of peak-hour-only services into the City the 176A, latterly a Monday to Friday-only service, was withdrawn without replacement in the devastating programme of 4 September 1982. As that date approaches RM225 (VLT 225) looks smart as it crosses Southwark Bridge on the last leg of its journey into the City. It was withdrawn from Upton Park in May 1986 and scrapped by Wigley that December. *Steve Smith collection*

Route 83
Converted from RM to crew M, 4 September 1982

Right: One of London Transport's longest inner-suburban services, the 83 had to tackle both heavily populated Wembley and the Hanger Lane Gyratory on its way between Golders Green and Hanwell Broadway. Its projection to Brentford disappeared under Reshaping, two years after RMs replaced Alperton's RTs on 31 December 1966. Southall's RM1068 (68 CLT) is captured in its home region on 27 June 1980, performing a garage run beyond Hanwell. Withdrawn from Putney in November 1987, it would pass to United Counties, eventually donning Stagecoach stripes before embarking on a new life in Mexico, where it was last reported serving as a nightclub in Cancun. *Geoff Rixon*

Right: A pristine RM354 (WLT 354) heads through Hendon on 20 June 1980. The relatively traffic-free streets would seem to underscore the suitability for OPO on at least some parts of the 83; the route had been converted on Sundays from 15 May 1971, initially with Merlins and subsequently SMSs, DMSs and finally Metrobuses, and it was the last-mentioned that took over from RMs full-time with effect from 4 September 1982, facilitating OPO conversion on 23 April 1983. Following withdrawal from Ash Grove in November 1985 RM354 would head to Sweden. *Geoff Rixon*

Route 105
Converted from RM to crew M, 4 September 1982

Left: The second route to assume crew M operation in the 4 September 1982 programme was, like the 83, a long and tortuous one which might have been better served in two parts; indeed, this is what would later happen, the Southall–Shepherd's Bush section now being the province of today's route 95. In its full extent to Heathrow Airport the 105 was one of the last dozen routes to retain RTs, gaining RMs only from 30 April 1978. At the time Southall and Shepherd's Bush shared the route in a 2:1 ratio, but the latter withdrew its participation on 31 January 1981. On 18 June 1978 Southall's RM948 (WLT 948) enters the airport bus station. It was scrapped in June 1987, three months after coming out of service from Camberwell. *Geoff Rixon*

Right: The Shepherd's Bush contribution to the 105 is represented by RM57 (VLT 57), pictured negotiating Southall's narrow streets on 14 October 1979. Three buses were shaved off the 105's run-out upon conversion to doored buses, 17 Metrobuses replacing 20 RMs, and all the new buses had to do on 23 April 1983 was discard their conductors. Six more transfers and an overhaul would characterise the subsequent career of RM57, which finally succumbed to the scrapman in February 1988. *Geoff Rixon*

Left: Greenford Broadway remains an easy pitch for the photographer wishing to hunt buses in large numbers, and such was the case on the morning of 19 October 1980 when Southall's RM1058 (58 CLT) crossed the lens. This bus was a long-stayer, coming out of service only with the one-manning of the 36 on 28 January 2005; in the intervening two decades its former haunt saw five changes of vehicle type and four of operator! *Geoff Rixon*

Route 93
Converted from RM to DM, 4 September 1982

Above: The 93, running then as now from Putney Bridge station to North Cheam under the able stewardship of Sutton garage, was another important route which had seemingly been forgotten when time came for it to upgrade from RT to RM. Routemasters took over this route only on 28 March 1976, lasting for six years until replaced by crew-operated Fleetlines of the B20 DM variety on 4 September 1982. OPO conversion ensued on 23 April 1983, since when a further three generations of bus have carried on operating over the same roads. Seen ascending Morden Road on its way to Morden and points north, Sutton's RM184 (VLT 184) had just days left in service; it would never work again, submitting to the cutter's torch at Goodwin's Carlton yard as 1983 drew to a close. *Steve Smith collection*

Route 101
Converted from RM to OPO T,
4 September 1982

Below left: Ploughing an undisturbed furrow from North Woolwich to Wanstead, the 101 could at one time field more than 60 buses and until 1955 was the last home of the Central Area STL. As London's docks contracted postwar and their East End workforce was resettled, the 101 found itself serving little but disused post-industrial wasteland, and its peak vehicle requirement dwindled accordingly. A flirtation with DMs lasted only from 26 February 1978 to 28 October 1979, and immediately prior to OPO conversion the route was operated by just 16 Upton Park-based RMs, one of which was RM1084 (84 CLT), seen sharing the North Woolwich stand with RML2390 (JJD 390D) — which had crept over from the 15 on 17 August 1982. Destined to be outlived by the RML by some 16 years, RM1084 was withdrawn in June 1987, and more recently North Woolwich has been abandoned by the 101 route. *Steve Smith collection*

Right: Days before the end of Routemaster operation on the 101 Upton Park's RM126 (VLT 126) takes the air at Wanstead. It would head to less salubrious surroundings in its new employment, replacing MDs at from the 63 Peckham, before one last overhaul took it to Victoria, where it ended its career in August 1986. The scrapyard beckoned two months later. *Steve Smith collection*

Route 102
Converted from RM to OPO M,
4 September 1982

Right: Always a peaceful meander across the suburbs of North London between Golders Green and Chingford, the 102 managed for most of its length to avoid the troublesome North Circular. RMs had formed at least part of the weekend complement since as far back as 1963, when Muswell Hill's Sunday-only share was converted, and by 24 January 1970 Palmers Green had sufficient RMs to spare on both Saturdays and Sundays, but during the rest of the week the 102 was overlooked as a candidate for modernisation, its RTs continuing until 1 January 1978. RMLs graced the Muswell Hill Sunday allocation between 1975 and 1978, when they were replaced by DMs; upon the 102's OPO conversion Muswell Hill withdrew, and Palmers Green replaced its RMs with Ms. In a rainy Silver Street during October 1981 RM5 (VLT 5) shows no sign of the showbus status that would later make it a favourite of several North London garages until its final withdrawal as the last AEC-engined bus in London service on 3 September 2004. *Geoff Rixon*

Route 104
Converted from RM/RML to DMS OPO, 4 September 1982

Above: This long-departed trolleybus-replacement route from North Finchley to Moorgate gained recognition for introducing the first RMLs on 8 November 1961 and would end its term of crew operation with the same type, though punctuated between 26 October 1975 and 31 October 1981 by six years of crew-operated Fleetlines. On 4 April 1982 RM952 (WLT 952) lays over at peaceful Finsbury Square, Moorgate. Withdrawn from Norwood in June 1986 and scrapped four months later, it only narrowly outlasted the 104, which was withdrawn in 1985 and had its northern section fused with the City portion of the 18 to form today's route 17. *Colin Brown*

Left: On the last day of conductors on the 104, 3 September 1982, RM1316 (316 CLT) strikes out down the Archway Road one last time. Transferred out of harm's way until one too many OPO conversions (that of the 237 at Hounslow) caught up with it, it would migrate to Spain in 1987 and settle in Alicante, in common with quite a few British expatriates of a certain age. *Steve Smith collection*

Route 106
Converted from RM to OPO T, 4 September 1982

Above: It gained notoriety as the route on which six years of OPO had proved such a catastrophe that Routemasters were restored in 1979, but the 106's restored dignity lasted only three years before the swing of the pendulum back to OPO on 4 September 1982, this time using the infinitely more reliable and amenable Titans. The first era of Routemaster operation, from Hackney and Poplar garages (the latter replaced by Tottenham in 1971, when the service between Poplar and Becontree was withdrawn), stretched from 2 December 1968 to 12 August 1972; the final act of the second began on 25 April 1981, when newly opened Ash Grove garage assumed sole control. Seen in May 1980 while still working from Hackney, RML2388 (JJD 388D) makes something of an unexpected jaunt away from the 6 to the 106's roads in Clapton. Many years later, it would end up with CentreWest's Westbourne Park garage for routes 7 and 23, finally coming off service in April 2004 and passing into preservation in Hampshire.
Steve Smith collection

Route 187
Converted from RM to OPO M, 4 September 1982

Above: A complicated slog northwestward into Metroland as far as South Harrow station, the 187 was converted to RM operation full-time on 23 February 1975, though weekends had seen Routemasters running since April 1964, Alperton and Middle Row garages being joined from 1970 by Stonebridge. This last closed on 15 August 1981, together with Middle Row, which passed its participation to the newly-opened Westbourne Park garage. OPO conversion saw the removal of the route's 187's Kensal Rise–Hampstead Heath section, though almost all of this has since been restored. During July 1977 Alperton-based RM1075 (75 CLT) ambles southeastward through Northolt, squeezing under Petts Hill Bridge with inches to spare. Passing to Mortlake on 4 September 1982, it would serve as a trainer before its sale to dealer C. F. Booth of Rotherham at the end of 1983. *Dave Brown*

Route 193
Converted from RM to OPO T, 4 September 1982

Above: Formerly known as trolleybus route 693, bus route 193 retained the 'round the corner' facility that enabled Barking to be served via Ilford on the buses' path from Hornchurch and Romford. The 193's Routemaster era had to wait until its operating garage, Seven Kings, was reconstructed to dimensions able to support Routemasters, Saturday services being converted from RT on 28 February 1976 and the rest of the route (there being no Sunday service) on 19 March 1977. RM662 (WLT 662) is illustrated at Romford Market on 8 September 1979; this bus would end its career at Elmers End in September 1985, thereafter passing to Wigley's for scrapping. *Colin Brown*

Above: RM2195 (CUV 195C) passes through Hornchurch on its way to Barking on 15 September 1979. It is curious why the cross-Romford link from east to west has not been revived in any form since the truncation of the 193 from 4 September 1982; one-manning saw it reduced to a vestigial shuttle service operating no further west than Romford Market. Withdrawn from Palmers Green in February 1988, RM2195 would donate its components to fellow vehicles at United Counties. *Geoff Rixon*

Route 196
Converted from RM to OPO T, 4 September 1982

Left: On 27 March 1971 the 196, from that date running between Euston and Norwood Junction, lost its Camberwell-based RTs for RMs. Having already lost its Tufnell Park end upon conversion to Routemaster, the route was further truncated at Brixton from 5 January 1974, having the peak vehicle requirement to just seven buses operated by Norwood garage. Stockwell took over on 25 April 1981, and the OPO conversion transferred the route back to Camberwell. Numerous allocation and type changes have ensued in the subsequent quarter century, and the 196 has been extended northwards once again. RM28 (VLT 28), with blank pink panels plastered over a time-expired pair of advertisements on either side of the blind box, is seen at Norwood Junction towards the end of RMs on the 196. It would transfer from Stockwell to Thornton Heath in June 1985, there to live out a further five months before withdrawal in November. It was broken up to provide spares for Clydeside's incoming Routemasters. *Steve Smith collection*

Route 229
Converted from RM to OPO DMS, 4 September 1982

Right: Picking around the southeastern perimeter of Greater London along the Bexleyheath–Sidcup corridor, the 229 was converted from RT to RM on 21 May 1977, from which date it was altered to run between Erith and Farnborough and was operated solely by Sidcup garage. Perhaps Sidcup's most famous Routemaster was RM8 (VLT 8), which was finally released to service by Chiswick's Experimental Department in 1976 and is seen rounding Orpington war memorial on its way to Farnborough on 21 May 1978. The tenure of Routemasters on the 229 was to prove short, as the route was selected for OPO conversion in the great programme of 4 September 1982, which also removed the Farnborough extremity; on that date nine DMSs replaced 10 RMs on a slightly shortened route, themselves to be supplanted two months later by new Titans. *Geoff Rixon*

Route 58
Converted from RM to crew T, autumn 1982

Left: Trolleybus route 685 gave way to bus route 58 on 3 February 1960, the conversion allowing some of the first production RMs to enter service. Walthamstow and West Ham shared the honours, Walthamstow always being the junior partner, dwindling to weekends only on 16 June 1973 and pulling out altogether on 31 April 1981. When the Titans started arriving the 58 was running between Leyton and Canning Town, much of its service northwards to Chingford Mount having been switched to 1981-introduced route 158, and thus required just 18 RMs (as opposed to the 30 of 1978). RM96 (VLT 96), seen exiting Cann Hall Road shortly before its ousting by Titans towards the end of 1982, is an appropriate representative of West Ham's operation. It remained at that garage until May 1985, passing three months later to PVS and thence to Wigley's for scrapping. *Steve Smith collection*

FOUR

Fiddling while Rome Burns

FOR all the much-appreciated events celebrating London Transport's Golden Jubilee, beginning at Chiswick in April and culminating with the Aldenham Spectacular on 25 September, 1983 was very much a swansong for the old order. Ominous changes to London's buses were on the horizon, accelerated by the savings made by withdrawing the first 200 RMs the previous autumn. A further 300 RMs would depart the fleet by the end of 1983, four routes being converted to OPO outright. This took place on 23 April, three of the casualties coming from the new RM routes introduced on 4 September 1982: the 60 (Croydon) fell to DMSs, the 225 (Seven Kings and West Ham) to Ts, and, in an unfortunate twist due to Bromley's not operating any OPO double-deckers at the time, the 261 to LSs, with the promise of Titans as soon as stocks could be made available.

Another milestone was the near-completion of the conversion of night bus routes to OPO, routes N83, N90 and N92 all losing RMs during 1983 and the N81 being withdrawn on 29 October; due to the likelihood of attacks on crews at night, doored buses had gradually become the norm on most of these routes.

Where the presentation of the Routemaster fleet was concerned, Golden Jubilee Year saw four splendid versions of 1933 livery applied to RMs 8, 17, 1933 and 2116. Each was subtly different, and all were a credit to their painters and garages. A further large number operated in original condition as showbuses, with gold-leaf fleetnames and fleet numbers, and refitted with chrome headlight rings and full-depth air intakes. The icing on the cake was RM1983, painted in all-over gold and sent around the fleet as the ultimate ambassador for the organisation. Fifty years of age LT may have been in 1983, but it was to survive just 11 more as a bus operator, its decline presenting a sight disheartening for anyone proud of its traditional role in the greatest of capitals.

Route 60
Converted from RM to DMS OPO, 23 April 1983

Introduced on 4 September 1982 as a localisation of the 130 north of West Croydon as far as Streatham, the 60 allowed conductors to stay put on this section while the 130 and 130B were converted to OPO — but only for seven months; on 23 April 1983 Croydon RMs gave way to Thornton Heath DMSs, spare examples of which were used to one-man the 190 on Sundays as a portent of things to come. During April 1983 Croydon's RM2155 (CUV 155C) motors through Pollards Hill. A one-time Shillibeer Routemaster, it was used during 1979 from Alperton on the 83 and, after bidding farewell to the 60, would see further service at Holloway, from where it was withdrawn in November 1987. It was one of 40 RMs to make the journey to Sri Lanka, where it initially worked in and around the capital, Colombo. *Steve Smith collection*

Route 225
Converted from RM to OPO T, 23 April 1983

Above: Another localisation of 4 September 1982, new route 225 was designed to take the pressure off trunk route 25 at its eastern end, which until then stretched beyond Ilford out to Becontree Heath and even Dagenham, reaching a length which was proving untenable in the face of contemporary traffic levels. For their brief tenure the RMs were provided by Seven Kings (Mondays to Fridays) and West Ham (Saturdays and Sundays); flying the flag for the latter garage one weekend in March 1983, RM561 (WLT 561) heads for Becontree Heath. Two years previously this bus had worn 'silver ribbon' livery to mark the wedding of Prince Charles and Lady Diana Spencer; after vacating the 225 it would move on to Edmonton, being withdrawn from there in March 1985. The 225 was reabsorbed by the 25 in 1988, but the Ilford–Becontree Heath section was separated once again in 1993, taking the number 128. *Steve Smith collection*

Right: From its introduction the weekday 225 had during the morning peak projected south from Becontree Heath to the Ford works at Dagenham, where Seven Kings' RM1599 (599 CLT) is seen on 22 April 1983, the last day of such workings and of crew operation on this route in general. This bus was withdrawn from New Cross in November 1984, but the story would not end there. After 14 years in exile with Stagecoach, during which time it worked with Magicbus, East Midland and Bluebird Buses and received the registration YTS 820A, it came back to London to augment the 15 from Upton Park garage. This route was the first of the final 20 to go OPO on 30 August 2003 and RM1599 was exiled again, this time to southwestern France. *Steve Smith collection*

Route 261
Converted from RM to OPO LS, 23 April 1983

Above: Only seven months into its existence, on 23 April 1983, the 261 suffered some indignity when it was converted from RM to single-deck operation with Leyland Nationals, these being the only OPO buses on which Bromley drivers were trained since that garage discarded its DMSs in 1980. Seen departing the 1978-vintage Lewisham bus station on a sunny morning in April 1983, RM929 (WLT 929) would be withdrawn from Wandsworth in February 1986 and scrapped by Wigley that October. *Steve Smith collection*

Left: Bromley's RM574 (WLT 574) is resplendent in showbus condition as it passes its home garage on its way south to Orpington via Farnborough. One should remember that this bus's presentation, with gold underlined fleetnames and fleetnumbers to match, was the standard at the time this bus was new. Having forsaken Bromley for Clapton, it was withdrawn in March 1985 and scrapped three months later. *Steve Smith collection*

Route 140
Converted from RM to OPO M, 23 April 1983

Left: Winter slush adorns Harrow Weald's RM1115 (115 CLT) as it works through Queensbury on 16 January 1982 during a particularly chilly winter, the likes of which London tends not to see any more. Crew-operated Metrobuses filtered into Harrow Weald in the early months of 1983, shedding their conductors on 23 April and making this garage all-OPO. This section of the long and busy 140 was swapped with the 114 upon OPO conversion, while RM1115 would proceed to Stamford Hill. Following withdrawal in November 1987, upon the OPO conversion of route 253, it would be exported to Sri Lanka. *Geoff Rixon*

Right: One of London's longest routes, until a very late stage the 140 allowed passengers entering Britain through Heathrow Airport the privilege of seeing RTs still in service, but after the type's ceremonial farewell from Harrow Weald garage on 15 July 1978 RMs were the staple fare all the way out to Mill Hill Broadway. An extension on Sundays to Mill Hill East was provided by three RMLs from Hendon. Harrow Weald's pride and joy during Jubilee Year was RM855 (WLT 855), seen in Heathrow's bus station shortly after midday on 17 January 1983. This bus would be kept in showbus condition by its next-but-one garage, Clapton, but lasted there only until June 1986, after which it was sold for scrap. A later shot of it working from Stamford Brook can be found on page 63. *Geoff Rixon*

Route 33
Converted from RM to crew M, 25 June 1983

Left: Withdrawn London bus routes almost never come back, but the 33 proved to be an exception. The Hammersmith–Hounslow service was swallowed up in 1958 by the more powerful 73 but on 31 December 1966 was reintroduced in its original form after four years of the number's use in the East End. The 'new' 33 was scheduled for 22 RMs from Mortlake, and a decade and a half of increasing traffic levels along its Upper Richmond Road routeing ensured that its peak vehicle requirement had reduced by only 2 by the time Fulwell joined in on 25 April 1981. Mortlake, though possibly London Transport's most admired garage for the cosy nature of its small allocation and the superb upkeep of its buses, could not be expanded and was closed on 25 June 1983; Fulwell garage, its contribution to the 33 having been converted to crew M four months after it gained a share of the route, now took on the remainder. The only Routemaster ever to appear thereafter on the 33 was RM254 (nowadays the property of this book's principal photographer), which on 1 February 1985 was loaned from Norbiton to Fulwell to perform the route's last crew journey. In happier times — during March 1982 — Mortlake's RM1354 (354 CLT) is seen in Richmond Bridge Road. This Leyland-engined Routemaster was withdrawn from Camberwell in February 1985 and scrapped that August by PVS of Barnsley. *Geoff Rixon*

FIVE

Calm before the Storm

JUST two OPO conversions marked 1984 — but more than 300 RMs departed the fleet. This was due largely to the deployment of almost all of the 1984 order for 240 Titans on crew routes. This process began on 2 March with the 86 at Seven Kings. As with the 40 at Poplar and the 69 at West Ham, its Titans were older examples cascaded, but the 161 at Plumstead and Sidcup, the 176 at Walworth and the 208 at Catford all used new buses. The Metrobus, though increasing in number by only 150 during 1984, was also a part of the process, displacing RMs from the 260 at Willesden during May, while new examples aided in the conversion of the 133 to doored buses during the autumn by releasing DMS from the 50 and 95. Meanwhile, DMSs in crew mode began displacing the large complement of RMs running on the 77A from Stockwell and the 190 from Croydon. However, it was the summer of the Titan as the last examples of the final order poured into South East London. Off came the 141's RMs at New Cross (though those from Wood Green would continue until the route's OPO conversion), followed by the last remaining RMs on the 180 worked from Catford (Plumstead's having already gone in 1981), the Catford and Bromley allocations on the 47 and, finally, the last Routemasters at Bromley in October, when the 119 and its Sunday-only 119B counterpart gained crew Ts.

The two OPO conversions mentioned were both effected on 27 October, and both were on Sundays only — firstly the 1A, a Sunday-only route introduced on 20 April to channel the 1's passengers to the attractions of Greenwich, and secondly the 141, the only segment of which to run on that day was the northern portion operated by Wood Green. At night, the last vestiges of RM operation disappeared from the N93 with its OPO conversion on 27 October.

Route 86
Converted from RM to crew T, spring 1984

Far left: In one form or another, through the years of LTs, austerity Guys, RTLs and then RTs, the 86 had been plying the Romford Road between Stratford and Romford (with extensions at either end) for generations by the time RMs were phased in. Their debut was not until 28 February 1976 — very late for such an important service, owing to the need for Seven Kings garage to be reconstructed to admit longer and wider buses. Upton Park's Saturday-only share had paved the way since 1970, this subsequently being upgrading to RML and lasting thus until 4 September 1982. RML2548 (JJD 548D) demonstrates its extra capacity on its way through Romford Market on 8 September 1979. Despite ending up at Brixton garage on what became the last Routemaster route (159), it was withdrawn in March 2005, nine months before the end. *Colin Brown*

Left: RM10 (VLT 10), allocated to Seven Kings, heads through Stratford on 16 August 1980. For many years the 86 continued west to Limehouse, and the decision by planners to remove this section on 4 September 1982 caused outcry sufficient to prompt it reinstatement from 23 April 1983, by which time the peak vehicle requirement had actually increased, to 26. On the same date another Saturday-only share was introduced, this time from West Ham, and it was this garage that maintained an RM presence on the 86 while the Seven Kings majority completed its conversion to crew T during March 1984. OPO conversion was effected on 2 February 1985. Overhauled in September 1981, RM10 was outshopped to Merton, from where it was withdrawn in May 1985. Six owners later, it can currently be found doing film work; now registered XFF 258, its most recent public appearance was at Routemaster 50, by which time it had been painted white with black spots to publicise the film *102 Dalmatians. Geoff Rixon*

Left: No account of the Routemaster during the 1980s would be complete without a tribute to the marvellous 1933-liveried quartet of RMs that were so painted to commemorate the 50th birthday of London Transport in 1983. RM2116 (CUV 116C) was Seven Kings' showpiece and by 1983 could work no other route than the 86, being seen that July heading west on its way to Limehouse. Although retired in May 1984, it has remained in this livery ever since and is a regular at rallies. *Geoff Rixon*

Route 69
Converted from RM to crew T, spring 1984

Above: Introduced on 3 February 1960 to replace trolleybus route 669, new bus route 69, running between North Woolwich and Stratford, was worked by 21 RMs from West Ham garage. Further trolleybus replacement one stage later saw the route projected over the 699 to Chingford Mount, while Chingford station was reached 7 September 1968, on which day a minority Leyton allocation was introduced. During the summer of 1971 there was a Poplar contribution on Sundays, but no other garage challenged the existing pair other than when new route 269 took over the 69 north of Walthamstow Central in 1973; when that ceased in 1976 Walthamstow was given a proportion of the 69. On 11 October 1981 a freshly-overhauled RM112 (VLT 112), one of 17 West Ham RMs allocated at the time, passes through Stratford. Aldenham's renowned treatment would buy this bus only two more years of service; it was withdrawn in January 1984 and scrapped that July. On 4 September 1982 the 69 was retracted to Chingford Mount, and West Ham garage, once more working alone, would receive crew Titans several months in advance of the OPO conversion on 2 February 1985. *Geoff Rixon*

Left: Representing the West Ham allocation of the shorter RM type is RM199 (VLT 199), passing through Walthamstow on 28 April 1980, a month after its fourth overhaul. It would transfer to New Cross the following February, after which its fifth and final overhaul at the turn of 1983/4 took it to Sidcup; when RM operation at that garage ceased at the close of 1985 it passed to Camberwell, remaining there until December 1987, when it was sold to PVS. *Geoff Rixon*

Route 161
Converted from RM to crew T, summer 1984

Right: The onward march of the Titan into South East London during the summer of 1984 soon enveloped the 161. The Plumstead allocation's crew MDs had already been replaced by Titans at the beginning of 1983; the Sidcup share remained RM until mid-1984, OPO conversion not being effected until 2 February 1985. Sidcup was the final posting of RM770 (WLT 770); in this July 1982 view taken at Mottingham the first coat of showbus cream has already been applied to the cantrail. The bus made it into the last six weeks of its home garage's final crew route, the 21, before succumbing to withdrawal in December 1985. It saw further service in Scotland with Kelvin Central at the dawn of deregulation but was broken up in 1991. *Geoff Rixon*

Left: The minority Sidcup allocation on the 161, which by 1983 was allocated just six RMs alongside Plumstead's 13 crew Titans, branched off at Chislehurst to reach their own garage. Chislehurst War Memorial is where we see Sidcup's RM301 (WLT 301) making this turn on 8 March 1983, when the trees in this surprisingly rural-appearing enclave of South East London had yet to regain their spring foliage. The bus remained at Sidcup until February 1985, when it was sold for scrap. *Geoff Rixon*

Route 40
Converted from RM to crew T, summer 1984

Right: Poplar's RMs had all gone by the time of its closure on 2 November 1985, the 40 being the garage's last crew route. It had received RMs on 27 January 1965, the accompanying West Ham allocation following suit on 10 July 1966, both in replacement of RTLs. However, between 13 June 1970 and 22 April 1978 the 40 was Saturdays- and Sundays-only, the weekday service being the province of route 40A. Busplan '78 simplified such inter-worked routes, the resulting daily 40 being shared between Poplar and Camberwell. The latter withdrew on 25 April 1981, and by 1984 the 40 was scheduled for 18 buses and operating between Herne Hill and the Blackwall Tunnel. On 24 April 1980 Poplar's RM44 (VLT 44) has short-worked to Camberwell garage, as has Croydon's RM1583 from route 68. After withdrawal in May 1984 RM44 was lucky enough to see further service with not one but two of the more famous Routemaster operations outside London — Southend Transport (1991-3) and Reading Mainline (1994-8). *Geoff Rixon*

Route 260
Converted from RM to crew M, summer 1984

Right: Trolleybus-replacement route 260 had soldiered on with RMs since its introduction on 3 January 1962, with little change to show since its previous identity as route 660 other than the inevitable alterations to either terminus. Stonebridge, the operating garage before and after trolleybus days, was assisted until 1970 by Finchley (with Hendon participating on Sundays for a time) and joined in 1978 by Willesden, which took over outright on the closure of Stonebridge in 1981, and it was Willesden that started receiving Metrobuses to replace the RMs in mid-1984. OPO conversion on 2 February 1985 saw the 260's service south of Willesden garage sheared off entirely, though it has since recovered. RM42 (VLT 42) was allocated to Willesden between July 1977 and January 1982 and is seen on 25 August 1979 at the Hammersmith terminus of the time. After sale in January 1986 it became Strathtay Scottish SR13, finally being broken up in May 1990. *Geoff Rixon*

Below: RM664 (WLT 664) spent its first four years in unpainted condition, earning it the nickname of 'Silver Lady', but thoughts of saving weight by omitting paint were thankfully abandoned. By June 1980 the bus was onto its third, red-painted body and allocated to Willesden, being seen at the Hammersmith stand of the 260, out of sight of the Underground station just around the corner. RM664 would survive to within 18 months of the end of Routemaster service, retiring upon the 137's OPO conversion on 10 July 2004. *Geoff Rixon*

Route 176
Converted from RM to crew T, summer 1984

Left: For such a long and important trunk route that passed clean through the West End, route 176 hardly seemed a candidate for doored buses, but in June 1984 Ts took over to displace RMs from an eight-year tenure that had begun on 11 March 1976, when Willesden's share received the type, followed shortly by Walworth's. Willesden withdrew on 28 October 1978, leaving Walworth with 22 workings on Mondays to Fridays; there had been no weekend operation since the withdrawal of the Saturday service in 1969, and it would not return until 1987, two years after OPO conversion on 27 April 1985. In a 28-year career during which it saw service 14 London bus garages, RM66 (VLT 66) spent only a month based at Walworth, arriving from Willesden in February 1979 and transferring to Hounslow almost immediately; as can be seen from the chalked route number, full blinds were not even found for it. However, its short posting to Walworth is immortalised on 9 March 1979 in this view recorded outside its temporary home. During the autumn of 1983 it was in for overhaul, enabling visitors to Aldenham's open day to see the work in progress; four years later it was cut down to a single-decker tow bus, in which form it spent some time with BTS before passing into preservation. *Geoff Rixon*

Route 208
Converted from RM to crew T, summer 1984

Left: The 208 was definitely the senior partner of the 208/261 offspring of withdrawn route 94 after 4 September 1982, and, as intended, ran past the gates of its operating garage at Catford. Subsequent transfers to and from Bromley would make a mockery of this efficiency-related aim, but that was for the OPO era, which was set in motion on 2 February 1985, the intended Titans having already eased out Catford's RMs the previous summer. During March 1983 a gleaming RM1359 (359 CLT) has just emerged from the vestigial bus station at Lewisham and is picking up for the trip south. Retired from Bow in July 1987, it would be sold to a firm in Sicily. *Steve Smith collection*

Left: The passenger of today would be hard-pressed to find a combination of route 208, Routemasters and Surrey Docks station as shown on the blind of RM346 (WLT 346); the route operated north of Lewisham only on Saturdays, its RMs disappeared in June 1984, and the area is now known as Surrey Quays. Seen at Deptford on 30 June 1984, RM346 left London nine years and three months later, for its trouble re-registered SVS 615; however, as part of the short-lived drive to restore Routemasters to London's streets it would return in February 2003 and was active on the 159 on the last day of normal Routemaster operation, Friday 9 December 2005. *Steve Smith collection*

Route 180
Catford allocation converted from RM to crew T, summer 1984

Above: The 180's Abbey Wood and Catford allocations both received RMs on 7 December 1968, by which time the route was operating between Abbey Wood garage and Lower Sydenham. Abbey Wood's participation was transferred to the new Plumstead garage, with MDs, on 31 October 1981, and the Catford allocation was withdrawn on 16 February 1982, leaving the 180 all-Metropolitan, but on 4 September Catford was restored, this time operating just three RMs. This Lewisham High Street view of RM1229 (229 CLT) dates from September 1984, when the rule of RMs was coming to an end — Catford would receive crew Ts shortly before its second withdrawal from the route on 27 October, OPO conversion, with Titans from Plumstead, following on 3 August 1985. RM1229 would meet a premature end on 14 May 1992 when it caught fire at Hyde Park Corner while working from Victoria garage on route 22. *Steve Smith collection*

Route 47
Converted from RM to crew T, autumn 1984

Left: RMs first appeared on the 47 on New Year's Day 1966, when the Saturday and Sunday Dalston allocation was converted from RTL, but nearly a decade was to follow before the Catford and Bromley shares followed suit on 26 January 1975. In the interim a Clapton RM allocation had come and gone, and upon closure in 1981 Dalston gave way to Ash Grove, whose showbus RM1737 (737 DYE) — nowadays an exhibit at London's Transport Museum — was caught at Lewisham on 13 March 1982. That year's 4 September programme removed the remaining workings north of Shoreditch (and the last north-of-the-river participation), together with the service between Bromley Common and Farnborough. Titans in crew mode took over the Catford share in August 1984 (19 buses), the Bromley allocation of seven buses following in September. *Geoff Rixon*

Above: On 7 June 1980 Dalston's RM1982 (ALD 982B) was sufficiently smartly presented to draw photographers' attention from the open day being held at Catford garage (visible in the background). The bus would last until October 1986, when it was withdrawn from Stamford Brook; PVS's scrapyard beckoned and had pulled it to pieces by the following summer. *Geoff Rixon*

Right: The showbus craze, whereby several Routemasters were lovingly restored to original condition by staff working in their own time, is represented by Bromley's RM574 (WLT 574), captured at Bromley Common on 6 March 1983. Another view of this bus in showbus condition appears on page 30. *Geoff Rixon*

Route 119
Converted from RM to crew T, autumn 1984

Above: RMs had operated the 119 since 2 May 1976, but the Routemaster's time at Bromley came to an end during October 1984; following the conversion of the 47 the last of the Titans reached the garage in sufficient numbers to do away with the RMs on the 119 and its Sundays-only 119B derivative in advance of OPO conversion (of the former) on 27 April 1985. RM1077 (77 CLT) passes Bromley South station on 20 August 1984, having set off from Bromley North approximately five minutes earlier. It was withdrawn from Wandsworth in March 1987 and exported to Finland, specifically the Aaland Islands. *Colin Brown*

Route 119B
Converted from RM to crew T, autumn 1984

Left: Introduced in 1970, Sundays-only route 119B differed from the 119 only by virtue of making its way along Shirley Way rather than Bridle Road in Shirley on its way between Thornton Heath and Bromley North. The route's five RTs were replaced on 26 January 1975 by five RMs, these in turn giving way to five crew Titans on 16 October 1984. Rendered unnecessary by the simultaneous one-manning of the 119 and diversion of the 194 on Sundays to serve Shirley Way (as 194A), the 119B was withdrawn on 27 April 1985. Shirley Way is today the exclusive province of the 194, working daily. RM15 (VLT 15), seen on 11 May 1980 in Croydon, was withdrawn in December 1990 from Putney and scrapped in May 1992, but its registration outlived it, first on Metrobus M1315 and then on a staff car at London General. *Geoff Rixon*

Route 190
Converted from RM to crew DMS, autumn 1984

Right: A fairly sleepy route on the southern periphery of London, the 190 was late to lose its Routemasters and even then practised with Fleetlines for a few months before OPO conversion. Daily RM operation was introduced on 20 November 1971, though the operating garage at Croydon had used the type on the 190's Saturday service for the previous year and a half. The Routemasters' tenure was interrupted briefly in 1975 by a handful of Leyland PD3s hired from Southend Transport during a period of desperate shortages, but this 11 May 1980 shot in North End, Croydon offers us RM530 (WLT 530). The groundwork was laid for OPO when the Sunday service went over to DMS on 23 April 1983, and it was only a matter of time before the rest of the route followed suit, on 2 February 1985. Coincidentally, RM530 was withdrawn that same month from Enfield, being scrapped by PVS in May. The 190 was withdrawn in 1990, its roads handed over to a restructuring of the 50 (and nowadays covered by the modern 60). *Geoff Rixon*

Below: This May 1983 shot at West Croydon offers us probably Croydon's all-time best — showbus RM1000 (100 BXL). It had gravitated to this garage following overhaul in 1980 and was given the full showbus treatment in January 1982. Too valuable to lose to the Barnsley scrapyards, it was bought by a team of Croydon staff in June 1985, more than a year before crew operation finished at the garage. Still to be enjoyed at rallies, it operated as a guest bus on 3 September 2004, the last day of Routemasters on the 73. *Geoff Rixon*

Route 77A
Converted from RM to crew DMS, autumn 1984

Left: Like the 36 group, the suffixed route had become the major partner in the 77 family, the 77A diverging at Wandsworth to serve Wimbledon and Raynes Park (its projections to Worcester Park finally being axed in 1978); in town it proceeded beyond Aldwych to King's Cross. The 77A had received RMs on 15 December 1973 when shared between Stockwell and Merton; accordingly the former's RM1652 (652 DYE), travelling along the Wandsworth Road in June 1980, is a suitable example of the *status quo*. By 1981 the weekend service had been restored, and on 27 October 1984 Merton withdrew to concentrate on its own 77. As 1984 began to wane a still sizeable peak vehicle requirement of 35 buses on the 77A awaited the arrival of Fleetlines released to Stockwell from Abbey District, whose Holloway and Chalk Farm garages had finally got rid of the DMS type that year. RM1652 was withdrawn in June 1984 and scrapped in December. *Dave Brown*

Above right: The major casualty in the battle against car traffic was the ability of London's buses to serve relatively far-flung suburban termini direct from Central London. One such was Raynes Park, abandoned by the 77A on 23 April 1983; nowadays the closest to town passengers can get using one bus is Wimbledon or Tooting, where they have no choice but to add to the congestion already suffered on the Underground. Nine days before the 77A was pulled back to Wimbledon (and that only as a peak-hour extension from Wandsworth), Merton's RM1186 (186 CLT) lays over at Raynes Park. It survived the 77A's subsequent OPO conversion on 3 August 1985 and remained in service till July 1993, its final garage being Victoria. *Steve Smith collection*

Route 133
Converted from RM to crew DMS, autumn 1984

Right: A very busy route through the most heavily populated parts of South London, the 133 had been converted from RT to DM operation in 1973 and but was released from that torment in 1981, when Brixton garage's second batch of Fleetlines was needed elsewhere and former Fulwell RMs poured in to replace them on both this route and the 109. One of their number, RM776 (WLT 776), looks perfectly at home on the 133 as it finishes one of this route's southbound journeys to Streatham garage. However, with OPO increasingly an option following the implementation of service cuts as part of the Fares Fair fallout, the opportunity was taken to replace the 133's RMs by holding on to Brixton's DMSs after their routes 50 and 95 were converted to M operation in the latter months of 1984. RM776 was a victim of this *volte face* in October 1984, being scrapped before year's end. OPO conversion caught up with the 133 on 2 November 1985. *Geoff Rixon*

Route 1A
Converted from RM to OPO T, 27 October 1984

Above: Despite the frenzied allocation of Titans in crew mode to former Routemaster routes, only one route was converted to OPO in 1984 — the recently introduced Sundays-only 1A, which from 20 April picked up its parent's course at Oxford Circus before diverting at Deptford to terminate at Greenwich. New Cross and Catford shared the service. Subsequent changes to the 1 on 2 November 1985 reintroduced that route as OPO on Sundays, while the weekday service also now ran to Greenwich rather than Catford garage, enabling the 1A to be withdrawn. Seen at Greenwich on 16 September 1984, one of four buses operated by Catford on that day, RM1228 (228 CLT) would be withdrawn from Camberwell in September 1988 and sold to PVS the following month. *Steve Smith collection*

SIX

The Purge

SATURDAY 2 February 1985 saw the first of four sweeping OPO programmes during a year that would reduce the proportion of crew operation in London Transport from 75% to 52%. Routes 33, 69, 86, 141, 161, 190, 208 and 260 were already operated by doored buses, but the 4 and 76 were straight conversions from RM to M, the former at Holloway and the latter at Tottenham. On the same day the eccentric but popular shoppers' services K1 and K2, worked by Norbiton RMs since the closure of Kingston on 13 January 1984, were withdrawn. One of that garage's number, RM254 (now owned by Geoff Rixon), was lent to Fulwell to perform the last crew duty on the 33 on the night of 1/2 February. The remaining conductors on night bus routes finished that same night; the final Routemaster-operated journey was performed on 28 January by RM294, even though the route in question, the N29, had commenced with crew Ms.

On 27 April the 118 at Brixton was converted from RM directly to OPO M, while the 45's share of RMs was reduced by the introduction of a new Walworth crew T allocation. The 119 and 119B were already T-operated and had but to shed their conductors, while Bromley garage was rendered all-OPO by detaching its half of the 47 as new route 47A. Time-honoured route 23, a fixture into the East End for generations and itself the subject of a recent branding exercise, was withdrawn on 18 May, the planners having made a last-minute decision to switch the weight of the Tower service to the 15 and relegate its normal Bank routeing to new subsidiary route 15A. Upton Park RMLs gained yellow bands (and yellow roofs, in several cases)

plus copious advertising that would be expanded to several more Central London Routemaster-operated services in the years to come. That garage's five-bus share of the 5 remained solidly RML, while the majority West Ham share started converting from RM to crew T during the summer.

The year's third OPO sweep occurred on 3 August, taking RMLs off the 48 at Leyton in favour of Walthamstow Ts, while the 45 lost both its recent Walworth share and its residual Stockwell RMs for full-time OPO Ts from Camberwell. At Norbiton the 71 was converted from RM to OPO M, while at Stockwell the 77A's DMSs shed their conductors; further Fleetlines began gathering on the hitherto RM-operated 77 at both Stockwell and Merton. Trolleybus-replacement routes 243 and 243A, by the end of crew operation RML-operated from Tottenham, exchanged their Routemasters for OPO Metrobuses, while the 172, now running only on Mondays to Fridays out of Camberwell, was withdrawn outright. As autumn approached, 20 of the 1985 order for 335 Metrobuses commenced the conversion from RM of the Wood Green share of the 41, followed shortly by an allocation to Norbiton for the 65 and, intriguingly, to Sidcup for the 21, despite that garage's being in a solidly Titan-operating District. The New Cross portion of the 21, substantially smaller than that at Sidcup, received Titans to replace its RMs.

Saturday 2 November witnessed the fourth and final Routemaster purge of 1985. Routes 5, 40, 41, 133 and 266 were already doored, but the 63 had not seen a rear-engined bus since its last MDs departed on 4 September 1982. This time it was Titans that drove away the route's 30 allocated RMs from Peckham.

Route 4
Converted from RM to OPO M, 2 February 1985

Left: Although RMs had replaced the 4's DMs on 31 January 1981 after a seven-year tenure, the route's conversion from RM directly to OPO M represented doored buses' revenge: On 27 April 1981 Holloway's RM72 (VLT 72), freshly transferred from Cricklewood, reposes in the bus station at Waterloo, now a bus garage in its own right. Having gained a Leyland engine at its last overhaul, RM72 was higher up the line for withdrawal than most and was removed from New Cross in November 1984. After languishing in store for seven months in the former Turnham Green garage it was sold on to PVS. *Geoff Rixon*

Top right: Several 35mm frames and a couple of hundred yards from the previous shot, RM27 (VLT 27) sets off from Waterloo — but only as far as Farringdon Street. Transferred from Walthamstow to Holloway two days earlier, it had yet to have the 'HT' code of its new host applied. Upon withdrawal from Brixton in June 1991 it bequeathed its registration to Leyland Olympian L27. Today the cherished VLT 27 mark adorns Wood Green-based Volvo B7TL VLW27, but its original host perished at the hands of Wigley's scrapmen in June 1992. *Geoff Rixon*

Route 76
Converted from RM to OPO M, 2 February 1985

Left: A longtime RTW route working out of Tottenham garage, the 76 was converted to RML operation on 1 November 1965, but only six months later XA-class Leyland Atlanteans took over experimentally. One Routemaster remained allocated to the 76's roster — the one and only FRM. Once the doored buses had sloped off to the outer suburbs in January 1970 a permanent RM allocation was instituted. Under Stage 3 of Busplan '78 the northern arm was extended from Tottenham garage to Northumberland Park station. This is where RM98 (VLT 98) will be heading as soon as its crew, out of shot, return from their tea break at Waterloo on a chilly 29 December 1979 . A trip to Aldenham in 1980 would see RM98 outshopped to Holloway, where it remained following a final overhaul four years later. An accident involving a crane would end its service career in 1988, but it was repaired to serve as a trainer until August 1992. At the end of 1993 it was sold to a concern in Denmark, which lowered its roof to comply with local regulations. *Steve Smith collection*

Left: With declining demand through the City and along Horseferry Road to Victoria, the 76's Sunday service had withered so much that by 1983 it was fair game for one-manning, four Ms replacing three RMs from 29 January. The inevitable weekday OPO conversion followed on 2 February 1985. Here RM1314 (314 CLT) is seen passing through Waterloo on Saturday 16 April 1983. After withdrawal from Stamford Brook in December 1986 this bus would pass to K. & M. Gagg of Bunny, Notts, for use on its Sherwood Forester network. Converted to open-top, it was exported in 1999 to Bermuda. *Steve Smith collection*

Route 141
Converted from RM to OPO M (Wood Green) and from crew T to OPO T (New Cross), 2 February 1985

Above: Created on 8 November 1961, new route 141 was assigned 50 RMs to replace both trolleybus route 641 and bus route 179, resulting in a very long trek from Winchmore Hill to Grove Park. The partnership between Wood Green and New Cross garages endured, though the route was withdrawn north of Wood Green on 7 September 1968, and each garage's participation was gradually cut back into overlapping sections. On 19 November 1977 the 141 received DMs in order to allow the more important trunk route 29 regain Routemasters, RMs not being restored to the 141 until 8 April 1982; accordingly the visit of Shillibeer-liveried RM2204 (CUV 204C) to the 141 on 27 October 1979 was a pleasant surprise. This bus, based at Wood Green at the time, was scrapped in 1994, its final posting being to Leyton garage. *Steve Smith collection*

Left: The appearance of RMLs on the New Cross share of the 141 was very rare, as the garage could muster fewer than 10 examples for its small allocation on the 37; however, RML2580 (JJD 580D) wandered to the 141 one day in August 1984 and is seen at Grove Park; when it turns around it will be going no further north than Newington Green, leaving Turnpike Lane and Wood Green to a Wood Green-based bus. The New Cross share of the 141 lost its RMs first, receiving crew Ts early in the summer of 1984. RML2580 was withdrawn from service upon the one-manning of the second route 94 on 24 January 2004 and has since passed into preservation in Gloucestershire. *Steve Smith collection*

Route 266
Converted from RM to crew M, February 1985

Above: RMs operated new route 266 from its introduction in place of trolleybus route 666 on 3 January 1962 and stayed two decades. Stonebridge and Cricklewood were the initial garages, to be joined at various junctures by Willesden (from 7 September 1968, reduced to Sundays-only from 17 June 1972 and with RMLs from 26 January 1975) and Hammersmith (six buses Mondays-Saturdays between 17 June 1972 and 28 October 1978, thereafter Saturdays-only until 4 September 1982). The service beyond Cricklewood garage to Edgware was pulled back to Colindale in 1970 but later diverted to Mill Hill; both extensions became redundant when Brent Cross shopping centre opened on 31 January 1976, and the 266 has terminated there ever since. Cricklewood's RM27 (VLT 27) was intercepted leaving this location during December 1980; its career following its transferring to Holloway, four months after this picture was taken, is detailed on page 44. *Geoff Rixon*

Right: Halfway through a 266 journey to Hammersmith on 23 May 1981, Riverside's RM419 (WLT 419) swings around the turning-circle at the end of the spur into Willesden Junction station forecourt. It was withdrawn from Shepherd's Bush garage in December 1985, one month after the 266 was one-manned (on 2 November), and headed to Scotland to become Kelvin Scottish 1914. Fortune did not favour Scottish Routemaster operation for longer than its immediate short-term competitive purpose, and RM419 would meet the scrapman's torch in January 1995. *Geoff Rixon*

Route K1
Withdrawn, 2 February 1985

Above: The surprising thing about 'Shoppers' Express' services K1 and K2 was not that they were withdrawn but how long they lasted in the first place. The by then unusual concept of having a conductor on hand to help shoppers with their bags was a winner, and the routes, marketed imaginatively upon their introduction on 12 November 1983, became popular. Unfortunately the accountants of the time did not agree, and both services ceased on 2 February 1985. However, both were resurrected, albeit as minibus services, on 27 June 1987, since when custom has since grown sufficiently to require three successive generations of progressively larger-capacity single-deckers. Renowned as a showbus at Kingston, RM254 (VLT 254) had passed into the care of Norbiton garage by the time it was sighted in Surbiton in August 1984. *Geoff Rixon*

Route K2
Withdrawn, 2 February 1985

Below left: Companion route to the K1 from 12 November 1983 was the K2, operating on Tuesdays, Fridays and Saturdays between Kingston and Tolworth, mostly assisting the 216 through Berrylands but, like the K1, allowing hitherto unserved Surbiton Hill Road a bus service. Like RM66 on page 37, RM19 (VLT 19) was also in works during the Aldenham Spectacular of 25 September and was outshopped to Kingston straight away, being seen in Surbiton Road on 2 December. Transferred to Norbiton upon Kingston's closure on 13 January 1984, it left that garage when route 65 lost its RMs at the end of 1985. Its final garage was Victoria, from where it was withdrawn in September 1987, scrapping at PVS ensuing during the autumn of 1988. *Geoff Rixon*

Above: RM23 (VLT 23) was the K2's bus on Saturday 3 December 1983, and this nearside view in Penrhyn Road allows us to see the 'Shoppers Express' slipboard carried. RM23 also moved on to Norbiton garage, four more postings following before conversion to a driver trainer, after which it received the most improbable registration LGH 31T, on account of its identity having been mothballed while on the works float and not reactivated until 1979! Upon sale to Reading Buses it gained JFO 256, which mark it retained when bought back by TfL to work on the 13 for Sovereign. However, it would not see the last day of conductors on this route (21 October 2005) and was sold by TfL after a period in storage at London United's Tolworth garage. *Geoff Rixon*

Route 118
Converted from RM to OPO M, 27 April 1985

Left: Another straight switch from crew Routemaster to OPO Metrobus involved route 118, which lost its conductors on 27 April 1985. For some time it was shared between Streatham and Brixton garages, the former having introduced RMs first, sparing some of its existing stock on Saturdays only from 17 June 1972, the rest of the route following on 14 December 1975 and Brixton taking sole responsibility from 28 October 1978. Throughout, the 118 ambled unruffled between Clapham Common and Morden, RM1587 (587 CLT) being seen *c*1981 in Cavendish Road after crossing the A24 junction just south of Clapham Common. Withdrawn from Holloway in February 1987, the bus would be scrapped three months later. *Steve Smith collection*

Route 23
Withdrawn, 18 May 1985

Right: For all but the last eight years of its life an East End fixture, the 23 ended up migrating westwards, absorbing neighbouring routes. RMs were early to the Poplar allocation on 11 November 1959, Barking following suit on 1 March 1964. Myriad garage reallocations ensued, such that by 1970 Upton Park and West Ham were in joint control. Barking's surviving Sunday participation reverted to RT on 18 July 1970 and the Sunday service was one-manned from 20 April 1974, with DMSs. During the week the 23 was converted to RML operation between 28 February 1976 and 19 March 1977, and in 1978 it was projected from Aldgate to Farringdon Street. On 25 April 1981 it was further extended to Oxford Circus, additionally reverting to crew operation on Sundays, and its final alteration, on 4 September 1982, took it all the way to Ladbroke Grove, the roads east of East Ham being left to the 5. At its end the 23 was operated by 17 Upton Park RMLs, along with just four buses from Poplar on Saturdays. One of the latter garage's allocation on 3 May 1980 was RM141 (VLT 141) leaving Aldgate. It would be removed from Clapton in December 1986 and make a final journey to the scrapyard. *Geoff Rixon*

Left: Pictured on the opposite side of the Aldgate roundabout on 27 September 1981 is RM25 (VLT 25), allocated to West Ham. This garage's share of the 23 had been officially RML since 1976, but on Sundays, as here, four RMs were allocated. RM25 had a long career, spending its final year in the brown, cream, yellow and black livery of the Great Northern Railway's horse buses and being withdrawn only in August 2005, some four months after its final route, the 19, had been one-manned. Still in its special livery and now reunited with its original registration (after a year as 855 UXC), it is now owned by Blue Triangle and during 2006 was used on that operator's Sunday excursions in Essex. *Geoff Rixon*

Left: In the 1980s London Transport was exploiting the new science of marketing to win over passengers who probably never perceived buses as a product to be bought and sold. During 1984 Upton Park RMLs on the 23 were treated to advertising that also extended to the route's bus stops and shelters. However, despite having carried out considerable work to brand the 23 as a route for tourists, on 18 May 1985 the planners wiped it out and transferred its routeing to the 15. Captured at Ladbroke Grove on 6 May 1985, RML2450 (JJD 450D) would be one of the 8's contingent at Bow until just before the end on 4 June 2004. *Steve Smith collection*

Route 45
Converted from RM/crew T to OPO T, 3 August 1985

Right: Descended from tram route 34, bus route 45 branched out at either end from its original Farringdon Street–Battersea remit. By the time RMs arrived on 23 June 1966 it had seen off RTLs, RTWs and Clapham garage and was shared between Chalk Farm (within reach of the Hampstead Heath terminus of the time) and Walworth, the latter in the majority. Chalk Farm withdrew on 8 January 1972, taking its buses to new route 46, but Walworth would not work alone for long, gaining Holloway as a partner on 28 October 1978. On that day the 45 was converted to DM operation, but RMs were to return on 25 April 1981. The Fleetlines' unreliability saw Routemasters making frequent stand-in appearances, as demonstrated by Walworth's RM12 (VLT 12), espied beneath the grand arches of Stockwell garage during July 1980. Stockwell would get its first turn on the 45 only on 27 October 1984, pulling out again on 27 April 1985, which day saw Walworth's allocation converted to crew T in advance of the OPO conversion on 3 August. RM12 finished its service days at Enfield in September 1987, leaving its registration to a coach-seated Metrobus and heading off to Southend Transport. In the subsequent ownership of BTS, its final act was to sacrifice its components to keep the 13's RMLs operational. *Geoff Rixon*

Route 48
Converted from RM to OPO T, 3 August 1985

Below left: The routes between Shoreditch and Clapton have frequently been subject to swapping from the Dalston Junction corridor to the more direct route via Hackney Road and Cambridge Heath. Such was the case with the 48, introduced on 7 September 1968 to link London Bridge and Whipps Cross via the routeing of the 38A (withdrawn) and 35 (diverted to run via Cambridge Heath instead of Dalston). Sunday RMs were introduced on 16 January 1971, and on 15 May that year the whole service was converted to RML, all from Leyton garage. Comparative peace and quiet ensued, the next change not occurring until 31 January 1981, when the RMLs were switched to the 55 and RMs returned. On 16 May 1982 a pair of fitters confer about a problem affecting RML2611 (NML 611E) at Walthamstow Central. It would seem that no long-term harm had been done, for the bus went on to complete another 22 years' service, culminating with the 73's OPO conversion at Tottenham on 4 September 2004. *Colin Brown*

Below right: A late exchange of termini with the 55, from 26 February 1983, saw the 48's Whipps Cross objective swapped for Walthamstow Central station. Feelers towards OPO were made when the Sunday service succumbed on 2 February 1985 (replacing the RMLs that had filtered back at weekends), but as Leyton then had no OPO double-deckers Walthamstow had to step in, and full OPO conversion on 3 August that year necessitated the transfer of the weekday service as well. A month before the end of crews on the 48 RM752 (WLT 752) flies up the Lea Bridge Road with much less traffic to contend with than this busy thoroughfare sees today. In 1986 this bus was converted to open-top by the Original London Transport Sightseeing Tour unit at Battersea to amble around the West End landmarks at a civilised pace. After 15 years on such work RM752 moved on but remains extant with Quantock Motor Services of Wiveliscombe, Somerset. *Steve Smith collection*

Route 71
Converted from RM to OPO M, 3 August 1985

Left: Introduced in 1950 as a local service connecting the new Ham estate with Richmond and Kingston, the 71 would not receive RMs until as late as 4 March 1978, after 15 months of STLs and 26 years of RTs. Following conversion to Routemaster it became the province of 14 RMs from Kingston garage, operating between Kingston and Leatherhead. Much of 1979/80 was spent as a shuttle run operating on both sides of the infamous Petersham Hole, a cavern formed by subsidence, which was supposedly repaired but quickly returned. On 31 March 1979 the 71's roads south of Surbiton were handed to RF-operated route 265, but on 27 September 1980 this route was withdrawn, allowing the 71 to resume its path as far south as Chessington Zoo. This is where Kingston's RM437 (WLT 437) was headed on 5 September 1983, but passengers could not be blamed for getting off at the stop at the bottom of Star and Garter Hill and venturing into the arguably more tempting Richmond Park. RM437 would not survive to transfer to Norbiton, coming off service in October 1984 and being reduced to its fundamentals by PVS before Christmas. *Geoff Rixon*

Left: Kingston's RM791 (WLT 791) heads north through Surbiton on 12 June 1983, Richmond its goal. The 71 was transferred with its RMs to Norbiton upon the closure of Kingston garage, on 14 January 1984. RM791 was to finish its London career allocated to Stamford Brook, being withdrawn in June 1986 when displaced from the 27 by a Metrobus; before autumn was out it had become one more of the hundreds of Routemasters broken up at Barnsley. *Geoff Rixon*

Right: As was the case with many Routemaster services during the 1980s, the path to OPO was paved by converting the Sunday service first and seeing how it performed. The 71's Sunday OPO service had developed independently from its parent since introduction on 2 January 1971, using RFs until 1977, BLs until 1982 (barring a two-year period when the 71 did not run on Sundays at all) and then LSs. When two Ms were introduced on Sunday 5 February 1984 they had to be routed northbound via Park Road in Norbiton, and this routeing was eventually applied to the rest of the 71 when further new Ms converted the route to OPO on 3 August 1985. Personifying happier days is none other than RM254 (VLT 254), whose owner photographed it during May 1985 at Surbiton with an eye to its purchase following its release from the 71. It has been maintained in the same outstanding condition ever since, and is to be seen at rallies the length and breadth of Britain. *Geoff Rixon*

Route 77
Converted from RM to crew DMS, 3 August 1985

Left: On 13 May 1979 Merton's RM161 (VLT 161) glides down Whitehall on a garage journey that will leave the line of route at Tooting Broadway and make a sharp right turn to its base in Colliers Wood High Street. The 77, for all its important trunk-route qualities, would not be upgraded from RT to RM until 15 December 1973, following which a contraction in 1981 removed the section south of Tooting and on to Wallington. A leg introduced to Streatham lasted just beyond the OPO conversion on 1 February 1986, which removed the conductors from the DMSs that had been filtering slowly onto the route since the summer of 1985. Despite being transferred away after overhaul in April 1981 RM161 would return to Merton for its final three years, being taken out of service in August 1985 when the 77 was converted to crew DMS operation. PVS took charge of the bus, reducing it to pieces. *Geoff Rixon*

Above: In June 1984 Merton's RM492 (WLT 492) speeds down Garratt Lane in Earlsfield on its way to Tooting Mitre. It did not last the year, being withdrawn in December and despatched immediately to the breakers. Prior to 1982 the 77 group could field an A, B and even a C suffix, according to which bridge was crossed on the southwest–northeast path. The 77 itself used Westminster Bridge. *Geoff Rixon*

Right: Earlsfield is also the location for Merton's RM441 (WLT 441), seen a hundred yards further up Garratt Lane than its sibling. Since the extensive changes of 25 May 1991, by which time the 77 had been OPO for more than five years, the 77 has not crossed any bridge at all and now serves Waterloo via York Road; the 77A (now renumbered 87) has been similarly pruned. RM441 was withdrawn in October 1985, going on to serve with Clydeside Scottish (1987-9), Western Scottish (1989/90) and Black Prince, of Morley, Leeds (1990-8), before being reclaimed by Transport for London for renewed service on the 13 (2001-5). *Geoff Rixon*

Route 243
Converted from RML to OPO M, 3 August 1985

Above: Stage 10 of the trolleybus-replacement programme was executed on 19 July 1961, replacing the network run by Edmonton and Holloway garages. As part of this scheme paired routes 543/643 were replaced directly by RM-operated bus route 243 over the same roads between Wood Green and Holborn Circus, RMLs taking over from 13 June 1970. The route's garage allocations fluctuated during the Routemaster era, Stamford Hill (1961-81) being complemented by Wood Green (1966-70) and Tottenham (1971-85). A change from the usual RMLs one day in August 1980 brought out one of Stamford Hill's splendid RCLs shortly after their reintroduction to stage service; these buses were normally restricted to the 149. RCL2240 (CUV 240C) at Stamford Hill Broadway shows the advantages of the full-width blind that was eventually adopted for the Metrobuses and Titans (and which is inexplicably forbidden today). After four years on the 149 it ended up on the Original London Transport Sightseeing Tour, in the fullness of time becoming a convertible open-topper, with platform doors restored. Now that that role has ended it is still to be found as a promotional vehicle for a brewery. *Geoff Rixon*

Route 243A
Converted from RML to OPO M, 3 August 1985

Left: Trolleybus routes 543/643 ran Mondays-Saturdays only, the Sunday service diverting at Shoreditch to reach Liverpool Street, close to the Sunday market at Petticoat Lane. This variation, in trolleybus days numbered 649A, survived the changeover to buses, giving rise to the 243A, which was able to continue further to the London Docks at Wapping. Upgraded from RM to RML on 13 June 1970 the route fell back to Liverpool Street on 4 December 1971, but it remained in this form until final withdrawal in 2000 when the parent route, complete with its Sunday service, was extended beyond Old Street to Waterloo. OPO Ms replaced RMLs on 3 August 1985, Tottenham having joined the Stamford Hill allocation on 28 October 1978 and taken over entirely on 25 April 1981. Bright winter sunshine on 16 January 1982 allows an early-morning glimpse of Tottenham's RML2668 (SMK 668F) swinging out of Buller Road, Wood Green onto the stand at Redvers Road. The area behind the bus, once the location of Wood Green market, is now occupied by a cinema complex. Subsequently transferred away from Tottenham, RML2668 would return to that garage in August 2003, albeit only as a parts donor. *Geoff Rixon*

Route 172
Withdrawn, 3 August 1985

Above: Reduced from 4 September 1982 to a weekday-only fragment of its tram-replacement peak and shorn of its unique service north of King's Cross to Archway via Barnsbury, the 172 could by 1985 do nothing that the 196 and 109 couldn't do just as well, and the route was withdrawn on 3 August. RMs might never have worked the 172 at all had not the DMs been so recalcitrant: the Fleetlines were withdrawn on 3 June 1982 from both Holloway and Camberwell garages, and the 4 September cutbacks removed Holloway altogether. On 31 July 1985, Camberwell's RM1040 (40 CLT) heads south through Kennington. Stood down in November and stored at the old AEC works at Southall, the bus was pressed into service at Norbiton in January 1986 when it looked as if the 65 might have to retain RMs; after that it was sold to Kelvin Scottish, eventually being scrapped in December 1991. *Steve Smith collection*

Right: The 172 is at the end of its life as RM177 (VLT 177) passes under the railway bridge carrying Southern Region trains into and out of Waterloo. Nowadays another 172 operates not too far from the route of its its predecessor, having been introduced in 1992. RM177 lasted nine more months working from Camberwell, being withdrawn in May 1986 and despatched to Kelvin Scottish. Further adventures took it to Regal of Kirkintilloch, but it was scrapped in 1995. *Steve Smith collection*

Route 41
Converted from RM to crew M, autumn 1985

Right: For such a comparatively short route, the 41 has always been tremendously busy, carrying the densely packed population of the Tottenham and Hornsey areas to and from work, school and recreation. Accordingly, postwar extensions in two different directions had been retracted by 7 September 1968 to Tottenham Hale; the simultaneous withdrawal of the West Ham allocation along with the second of these extensions took away the first garage to operate RMs on the 41, but on the same day Tottenham introduced the type. A Wood Green allocation was introduced on 4 September 1982, and this garage took up the majority, ultimately receiving enough Metrobuses to take over the whole route upon its OPO conversion on 2 November 1985. However, in February 1980 the 41 saw a guest appearance by the last RM to remain in Shillibeer livery, Tottenham's RM2160 (CUV 160C), seen having decanted its passengers at Archway. This bus was withdrawn from Stamford Brook in November 1987 and retired to Sri Lanka. *Geoff Rixon*

Left: Looking immaculate on a sunny 18 June 1984, RM1270 (270 CLT) was photographed from exactly the same spot as the subject of the previous picture, some four years earlier. At the time allocated to Wood Green, this bus would leave the 41 for the 149 and 279 at Enfield, departing thence in April 1987 and submitting to the cutter's torch at Wigley's two months later. *Colin Brown*

Route 5
Converted from crew T/RML to OPO T, 2 November 1985

Left: Like the 106, route 5 was a route distinctly unsuited to OPO, at least with the earliest DMSs. With weekend partners 5A and 5B the 5 was RM-operated from the start, having replaced trolleybus route 665 on 11 November 1959. Allocations between Poplar and West Ham fluctuated, eventually settling in favour of the latter, which introduced RMLs on 1 February 1966. DMSs took over on 17 February 1971 but departed ignominiously 10 years and eight days later, to be replaced by RMs from West Ham, although the Sunday operation remained OPO until 23 April 1983. From 4 September 1982 Upton Park reintroduced RMLs to the 5, a daily quintet lasting right to the end of the second period of crew operation on 2 November 1985. Seen on Waterloo Bridge on 9 October of that year, an advertisement-free RML2642 (NML 642E) was by now one of very few Routemasters still to figure on the 5, West Ham's RMs having all been replaced by crew Titans ahead of the OPO conversion. Having ended its London career on the last day of the 8's conductors from Bow (4 June 2004), this bus crossed the Atlantic to Canada, where it now operates in Montreal with platform and staircase reversed. *Steve Smith collection*

Route 63
Converted from RML to OPO T, 2 November 1985

Left: King's Cross to Crystal Palace was the extent of route 63 when its first RMs arrived on 1 February 1961, and the termini remained the same upon one-manning 24 years later. Those first RMs furnished a minority Holloway allocation that was taken off in 1970, along with a weekend-only 63A, which since 1963 had probed further north to Hampstead Heath; otherwise the 63 was Peckham's responsibility. Peak vehicle requirements dwindled during the Routemaster years, from 36 RMs in 1970 to 27 in 1982. Between 1976 and 4 September 1982 the 63 was the home of the MD class of Scania BR111DH / MCW Metropolitans, albeit still crew-operated. The sunshine playing over the Old Kent Road on 21 August 1985 does little to divert attention from the weary state of Peckham's RM1823 (823 DYE), with radiator triangle missing and a large dent in the roof dome. Surprisingly, it would remain in service following the 63's OPO conversion, moving a mile down the road to New Cross, where fate caught up with it in May 1987. It was duly broken up by PVS, its components (minus, presumably, the scarred roof dome) being sent onward to Clydeside Scottish. *Steve Smith collection*

Route 21
Converted from RM to crew M/crew T, autumn 1985

Right: Hauling passengers up and down the Old Kent Road and A20 between Moorgate and Foots Cray, the 21 was still very much a substantial trunk route in 1985, when the inevitable conversion to doored buses was effected using an unprecedented same-garage mix of Titans and Metrobuses due to the lack of sufficient examples of the former chassis. When RMs replaced RTs on 1 March 1975 New Cross was allocated 18 buses and Sidcup 13, but Sidcup progressively gained the ascendancy, to the extent that by the time the 21's RMs started departing it could field 16 buses to New Cross's five. Pictured in April 1983, RM63 (VLT 63) exemplifies the Sidcup-allocated Routemaster and at that time could appear on the 161 as well as the 21. It had arrived from overhaul in December 1981 and was withdrawn in August 1985, to face the breakers the following month. *Geoff Rixon*

Left: The career of RM8 (VLT 8) almost warrants a book to itself. New in 1958, it was not placed in service until March 1976, after an amazing 18 years serving as the testbed for a variety of experiments carried out by the staff at Chiswick Works. The bus would only ever work from Sidcup, spending nine years there, and during Golden Jubilee Year was an appropriate choice to be treated to the marvellous recreation of the livery carried by London Transport's buses at the time of its formation in 1933. The bus maintained its connection with Sidcup following its withdrawal in March 1985, being purchased by a group of garage staff; this consortium, known as the RM8 Group, continues to maintain it in superb condition and allowed it to perform one of the special workings run in advance of route 8's last day with Routemasters during 2004. *Geoff Rixon*

SEVEN

Breaking Point

THE events of 1986 served as proof that there was now no compunction against removing crew operation from strictly Central London routes, regardless of the inefficiency this was causing to both boarding times and timetables; accordingly 1 February saw the 18, 21, 65 and 77 one-manned. The 65 very nearly escaped, having had to re-equip hurriedly with RMs from sales stock in order to release Metrobuses to rescue the situation at Southall, where two dozen buses had been destroyed or damaged in a fire on Christmas Day 1985. However, these rescued RMs became part of the first complement on the Round London Sightseeing Tour, which was splendidly relaunched on 22 March as the Routemaster-operated Original London Transport Sightseeing Tour. For once, RMs replaced Ms, and not the other way around! Meanwhile, the Tottenham-operated northern section of the 171 was separated on 1 February 1986 as the 171A, the 171 continuing from New Cross but soon to be taken over by crew Titans.

The year continued with a second OPO programme unleashed on 21 June. In the previous 10 weeks moves had been made to restock some of the affected crew routes with doored buses. In April the 37's RMLs gave way to Ms at both Clapham and Hounslow (though the six RMLs from New Cross were untouched until the end, when its allocation was removed), and the 35 at Ash Grove began receiving a mixture of Metrobuses and Titans as a large surplus of the latter type developed following heavy losses to tendering. Camberwell's share of that route went over to Titans. The 134 at Muswell Hill was already predominantly crew M by the time of its one-

manning, while peak-hour-only route 8A, RML-operated like its parent 8, had to be reallocated from Bow to West Ham in order to facilitate OPO with Titans. At Norwood the 2 was one-manned on 21 June, its parent 2B being curtailed at Baker Street to allow a partial OPO conversion, achieved by the introduction of new route 82.

Although by now on the fringes in LBL's OPO complement, DMSs still figured in the removal of RMs when crewed examples began taking over the 155 at Merton in advance of its OPO conversion on 25 October. Moves prior to this date saw the 27 at Turnham Green lose its RMs for crew Ms (leaving Holloway's share all-RM until the end), the surviving half of the 171 at New Cross gaining Ts, and most of the long trunk route 68 prepared for OPO (with new L-class Olympians moving into Norwood but RMs staying put at Croydon and Chalk Farm until the last day). At Westbourne Park crew Ms had seen off the 52A's RMs in advance of 25 October, but the parent 52 at Willesden underwent a straight switch from RM to OPO M on conversion day. So too did the 113, Hendon-operated and another lengthy trunk route, stretching from Oxford Circus to Edgware. The most important route to lose its conductors on 25 October was the 24, RML-operated from Chalk Farm but by the end already partially converted to a mix of crew M and T (again, with the latter type to prevail).

As the year drew to a close a start was made on converting routes 149 and 237 to crew M — the former shared by Enfield and Stamford Hill, the latter the last route at Hounslow to be worked by Routemasters.

Route 65
Converted from RM/RML/crew M to OPO M, 1 February 1986

Left: The introduction of crew Metrobuses to the 65 as the autumn of 1985 turned to winter really brought home how serious London Regional Transport was about cutting costs. The 65 had been the model crew route, ploughing the long furrow between Ealing Broadway and Chessington Zoo since time immemorial but converting to RM only on 19 October 1975. Extensions to Ealing (Argyle Road) and Leatherhead, at either extreme of the route, had withered away without detriment to the main service, and Norbiton garage could field 31 RMs on its own until Kingston was invited to join in from 31 March 1979. From 4 September 1982 the 65 was Kingston's alone, but closure of that garage on 14 January 1984 restored Norbiton in full. A curious move added a Hanwell share on Sundays only from 3 August 1985, introducing RMLs for the first time. Intercepted alongside Ham Common in July 1980, RM1979 (ALD 979B) was fresh out of works and allocated to Norbiton; it would have a long career, sidestepping withdrawal despite having a Leyland engine at this time. It was active on the 98 on its last day as a crew route, 26 March 2004. *Geoff Rixon*

Above: Quite why a Hanwell allocation was introduced to the 65 on Sundays with but six months of crew operation remaining is a mystery; presumably there was a surplus on the 207 at that garage and it made sense to find work for them reasonably locally. This late development, instituted on 3 August 1985, brought a scheduled RML element to a route on which longer Routemasters had in the recent past been strange visitors — always loaned, as it happens, from Hanwell. RML2275 (CUV 275C) speeds southwards through Surbiton on 16 October 1985. Later in life it would become the first RML to acquire plain upper-deck front windows — a feature it retained until withdrawal, from Camberwell on 5 November 2004. Sold via the great Ensign raffle, it now resides with a preservationist in Wolverhampton. *Geoff Rixon*

Right: Disaster struck Southall garage on Christmas Day 1985, fire breaking out on the one day its entire allocation of Metrobuses was within its walls; a dozen were destroyed, and replacements had to be diverted from the new deliveries intended to displace RMs from the 65 at the tail end of 1985. When 10 RMs were retrieved from Sales stock at Turnham Green and sent back to Norbiton to free them it looked very much as if the 65 would not go over to OPO on 1 February 1986 as planned; certainly RM84 (VLT 84), circumnavigating the Copt Gilders Estate in north Chessington on 16 January 1986, does not portend impending one-manning. Its eleventh-hour reprieve from withdrawal saved this bus's life: after salvaging the 65's honour (albeit briefly) it would go into the Original London Sightseeing Tour fleet as an open-topper. It continues to perform that role in Edinburgh, and now there's even more of it: in 1990 it was extended using an extra bay from a withdrawn compatriot and is now 32ft in length — even longer than an RML! *Geoff Rixon*

Route 134
Converted from crew M/RM to OPO M, 21 June 1986

Left: A long and busy route linking London's northern fringe at Potters Bar with its very heart at Pimlico, the 134 began receiving RMs on 15 July 1964 for its Holloway (J) and Muswell Hill allocations. The receipt of RMs at Potters Bar garage on 27 January 1965 completed conversion of the route from RT, but as with so many other overextended London bus routes fighting the inexorable growth of car traffic, only retrenchment could follow. The opening of the Victoria Line put paid to everything south of Warren Street in 1970, but a later rally in 1975 restored the 134 to Tottenham Court Road, where it continues to terminate today. Holloway withdrew on 25 October 1969, and on 15 December 1973 so did the Routemasters, replaced initially by crew-operated DMSs and then by DMs. Doored crew buses did not, however, find favour, and it is surprising how long it took for the 134 to revert to RM operation, which was executed on 4 September 1982; RM1069 (69 CLT) is seen heading south two weeks later. Believe it or not, this bus is still working from Potters Bar — albeit the premises of Sullivan Buses, which operator has owned it since 2000. *Geoff Rixon*

Left: Another Routemaster allocated to Potters Bar for the reversion of the 134 from DM operation was RM2114, also photographed on 18 September 1982 north of the GLC border. However, the 134's renaissance was not to last; on 23 April 1983 the 134 started falling back from London's northern perimeter, losing the Potters Bar allocation and all its service north of Barnet Church, its terminus when Metrobuses began infiltrating Muswell Hill's remaining 18 workings in time for the OPO conversion on 21 June 1986. RM2114 gravitated to Putney, from where it was withdrawn in October 1987; following a spell with Burnley & Pendle (with *EastEnders*-themed name *Wicksy*) it was exported in 1992 to Hungary. *Geoff Rixon*

Route 37
Converted from crew M/RML to OPO M/OPO DMS, 21 June 1986

Left: The 37 was perhaps the quintessential inner-suburban route, so eminently suited to RMLs it ran them for 20 years, although the garages and the sections of route they served between Hounslow and Peckham changed several times. When RMs replaced the 37's RTLs on 18 December 1962 Putney and Stockwell shared the roster, along with Rye Lane on Sundays. From 1 June 1966 the longer Routemasters take charge, and Rye Lane's closure on 22 March 1969 saw Peckham step in on Sundays (and daily from 17 April 1971 until 8 January 1972, when this garage withdrew altogether). New Cross gained a majority share from 11 October 1975, while Putney's allocation was transferred to Hounslow on 28 October 1978. One of the last-named garage's dedicated batch for the 37 was RML2609 (NML 609E), seen crossing Richmond Bridge on 6 September 1981. The final allocation change of the 37's crew era saw Stockwell withdraw on 25 April 1981 in favour of an allocation from the temporarily reopened Clapham garage, which was host to Norwood's crews (and adopted its N code) while their garage was being rebuilt. When Norwood's staff went home three years later, Streatham's people were exiled in the same manner, again bringing their own code (AK) with them. Two months before the introduction of OPO Clapham and Hounslow began re-equipping with crew Ms, but New Cross retained its RMLs until the conversion on 21 June. RML2609 survived into the 21st century and ended up at Westbourne Park, on whose route 7 it suffered an accident at Marble Arch on 10 December 2003, causing it to be written off. *Geoff Rixon*

Route 2
Converted from RM to OPO M, 21 June 1986

Right: The 2 of 1986 was not the north-to-south colossus that had so proudly hosted RM1 in 1956; repeated cuts and transfers of emphasis to the 2B had rendered it a sickly little remnant. Daily RM operation did not manifest itself until 14 June 1967, although the weekend allocations from both Stockwell and Cricklewood had used them for the previous three years; Cricklewood withdrew on 13 June 1970, taking its RMs to the new 26, which took over the 2's roads north of Golders Green. At the same time the section between Norwood garage and Crystal Palace was switched to the 2B, a Norwood/ Stockwell partnership that had been RM-operated since late 1966. In 1978 the 2 was diverted at West Norwood to the Rosendale, and the cuts of 4 September 1982 saw it withdrawn between Baker Street and Golders Green, that leg again propping up the 2B. Despite weekend workings by Victoria and Norwood during the 1970s, plus a further six months of Monday-Friday workings from Victoria between 27 October 1984 and 27 April 1985, the 2 at the end of crew operation was Stockwell's alone. A chance shot at Victoria one evening in January 1981 allows a comparison between the 2 and 2B, worked respectively by RM1566 (566 CLT) and RM1527 (527 CLT). The former was withdrawn in September 1982 and broken up by Booth's, but the latter lasted until 2003 in service at Upton Park, in between spells on loan to the BBC for use in *EastEnders. Geoff Rixon*

Right: Captured in the latter half of March 1986, RM941 (WLT 941) heads south through Tulse Hill, on the last leg of the 2 before reaching its then southern extremity at West Norwood. Although by 1986 the 2 had been relegated to a secondary aspect of the 2B, its revamping six years later as minibus route 322 would herald something of a renaissance, with significant extensions. But by the time that came to pass RM941 was long gone; the 2 was its final posting, and following withdrawal in August 1986 it was scrapped by PVS in February 1987. *Steve Smith collection*

Route 8A
Converted from RML to OPO T, 21 June 1986

Left: Commencing, like the 8, from Old Ford, route 8A took a left turn at Bank and crossed the Thames to terminate at London Bridge station. RMs arrived on New Year's Day 1965; contraction began on 25 October 1969 with the withdrawal of the weekend service. RMLs were introduced on 28 October 1978; by the end of its time as a crew route the 8A (reduced to peaks only from 28 July 1984) needed seven RMLs from Bow. Seen at Liverpool Street on 12 August 1980 is RML2329 (CUV 329C), which had last served at Northfleet before reclamation by London Transport. It ended its career at Clapton on the 38 in October 2004, a year before that route was one-manned. Since August 2005 it has been working for Absolute Charters in Halifax, Nova Scotia, Canada. *Geoff Rixon*

Route 35
Converted from RM to OPO M/OPO T, 21 June 1986

Right: The day RMs took over the 35, 7 September 1968, saw the route's long-established inner-Essex portion beyond Hackney to Chingford Hatch divided between new routes 48 and 235 plus new flat-fare OPO service W21. Hackney and Camberwell shared the honours, the former's allocation transferring upon its closure on 25 April 1981 to Ash Grove. On 23 January 1982 the route was extended the short distance to Clapton Pond. By the end of crews Ash Grove and Camberwell were still sharing the 35, while Walworth contributed a Sunday share from 3 August to 2 November 1985. Prior to OPO Ash Grove began phasing in a mix of Metrobuses and Titans (the latter ultimately prevailing), but Camberwell did not take additional Ts until 21 June. A previous Camberwell steed on the 35 was RM2194 (CUV 194C), espied inside its home garage on 9 March 1979. Withdrawn from Stamford Brook in September 1987, replaced on the 9 by an RML, it was scrapped that December. *Geoff Rixon*

Below: The return from the dead of RM7 (VLT 7) allowed the organisers of Routemaster 50 on 24/25 July 2004 to present all but one (RM2) of the first 10 Routemasters built. It had not lasted long enough to see out the 35, being withdrawn in August 1985 when the 172 was axed, but proof of its working on the 35, with the elegantly hand-painted 'Q' codes that survive today, was secured at Clapham Common on 5 May 1980. At that time it was carrying plain-windowed body B50, but overhaul in October 1981 gave it B542, a later body it retains today. *Geoff Rixon*

Left: Just across the street from the vantage-point of the previous photograph is Old Town, the Clapham Common terminus of the 35; upon OPO conversion it was extended a mile to the west to reach Clapham Junction. From its opening Ash Grove had been allocated RMLs to fulfil its share of the 6, and occasionally these would slip out on the garage's other crew routes, such as the 9 and 35; one such interloper — albeit at the eleventh hour — was RML2304 (CUV 304C) on 14 June 1986. This bus would not move far, going only a mile up the road to Clapton when Ash Grove was closed on 23 November 1991 and remaining there until 28 October 2005, the last day of the 38's Routemasters. *Colin Brown*

Route 27
Converted from RM to crew M, summer 1986

Right: The 27 survived for so long at its comparatively extended length perhaps by virtue of avoiding Central London's most pressured areas on its way from Richmond via Kensington, Notting Hill and Paddington to Archway, although both ends have since been snipped. Routemasters appeared relatively late, on 13 June 1970, which date also saw the removal of outer companion 27A. Holloway (J), Riverside and Turnham Green had broadly equal shares of this 38-bus service when RMs arrived, but retrenchment was inevitable. On 3 September 1971 the 'new' Holloway (HT, formerly Highgate) took over its namesake's share, Riverside withdrawing save on Saturdays (and completely from 1978). Fulwell chimed in from 17 September 1971, working the Sunday service that still ran beyond Richmond to Teddington; for its final year of involvement that garage provided crew Ms, finally withdrawing on 4 September 1982, when the remaining service beyond Richmond ceased. Surprisingly, from that date Riverside made a reappearance on Sundays — but not for long, as it closed on 25 June 1983, its share being operated by Shepherd's Bush until 27 April 1985. By that date the weekday service was provided by Holloway and Stamford Brook (which had replaced Turnham Green on 10 May 1980, retaining the V code), operating 10 RMs each. Metrobuses would filter onto the Stamford Brook allocation first, during the summer of 1986, but only upon one-manning on 25 October 1986 did they feature in the Holloway contribution. At Richmond bus station on 15 October 1978 stand RM1909 (ALD 909B) on the 27 and RML2554 (JJD 554D) on the 37; neither route serves Richmond any more, and their pitches at this terminus are now used by the 391 and 337 respectively. RM1909 was withdrawn from Cricklewood in October 1984 and has spent the succeeding two decades on the Canadian side of Niagara Falls; RML2554 ended its working life on the 12 on 5 November 2004, following which it was sold via Ensign's raffle to a preservationist in Berwick-upon-Tweed. *Geoff Rixon*

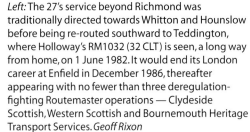

Left: The 27's service beyond Richmond was traditionally directed towards Whitton and Hounslow before being re-routed southward to Teddington, where Holloway's RM1032 (32 CLT) is seen, a long way from home, on 1 June 1982. It would end its London career at Enfield in December 1986, thereafter appearing with no fewer than three deregulation-fighting Routemaster operations — Clydeside Scottish, Western Scottish and Bournemouth Heritage Transport Services. *Geoff Rixon*

Left: With a patch of pink primer applied following repairs to the most vulnerable corner of its roof dome, showbus RM855 (WLT 855) demonstrates that no London bus is immune to out-thrust tree branches; the rest of it looks pretty splendid, however, as it passes through the long-gone Butterwick bus station at Hammersmith during September 1983, whilst attached to Stamford Brook garage. Its fate is detailed on page 31. *Geoff Rixon*

Route 155
Converted from RM to crew DMS, summer 1986

Above: Tram-replacement route 155 had long since abandoned its role as Embankment circular by the time RMs arrived at Merton on 15 December 1973, but Routemaster workings at weekends had been a feature since 1966, especially from Norbiton, which abandoned its share on 12 May 1973. A service from Wimbledon station up the busy Clapham Road to the Elephant & Castle, it had its Central London terminus altered from 27 October 1984 to Aldwych during weekday peak hours and on Saturday mornings. DMSs in crew mode were all in place in advance of the conversion to OPO on 25 October 1986. Mixed fortunes have been the 155's lot ever since, the route seeing an unsuccessful re-routeing to Vauxhall, complete withdrawal southwest of Tooting and two separate and equally ill-founded conversions to minibus operation. Back in July 1978 Merton's RM1918 (ALD 918B) is seen at the Elephant & Castle on its way to Wimbledon; withdrawn in September 1984 and exported to South Africa, it was thus spared the sight of the shopping centre behind it transformed from a ghastly green to an even more hideous shade of pink! *Geoff Rixon*

Left: At the Wimbledon end of the 155 on 23 June 1979, RM108 (VLT 108), another Merton bus, is in the Broadway, out of range of the traffic that eventually put paid to this route's ambitions in this part of South West London. The conductor has mistakenly wound up an intermediate blind for the 77A. RM108 underwent another overhaul in May 1981 and passed to Elmers End garage, which would be its final berth in London. Although withdrawn in June 1984, it would enter a life of preservation which continues today, retaining its (now very rare) Leyland engine to boot. *Geoff Rixon*

Route 68
Converted from RM to crew M/crew L, summer 1986

Left: A wearying north–south slog, the 68's goal was to transport passengers the 15 miles between Chalk Farm station and South Croydon garage, but nowadays the traveller wishing to make this journey would have to change buses twice. Having seen RMs on Sundays as early as 1963, the route was converted to full Routemaster operation on 7 February 1970, from Chalk Farm, Norwood and Croydon garages. Walworth had a Sunday share for five months in 1972, in which year Camberwell gained a weekend allocation; on 5 January 1974 the latter garage increased its participation to daily in lieu of Norwood, this situation being reversed on 27 October 1984 upon Norwood's reopening. Finally, Thornton Heath had an allocation on Sundays from 2 February 1985. Within five years of OPO conversion, the 68 could see DMSs, Metrobuses, Titans and Olympians in service simultaneously. But all that seems light-years away as a southbound RM46 (VLT 46) approaches Waterloo on its way to its home garage at Croydon on 27 April 1981. It was withdrawn from Victoria in July 1993, bequeathing its registration to Metrobus M1046; the mark now adorns London General's powerful Volvo B12FM recovery vehicle. *Geoff Rixon*

Left: If the photographer were standing at this spot in Station Road, West Croydon, today not only would he not be able to find any 68s; he would also risk being mown down by a tram! Back on 29 May 1982 Camberwell's RM1965 (ALD 965B) was a typical route 68 bus; it would spend the rest of its life based at that garage, OPO conversion of the 35 hastening its withdrawal in May 1986. It was scrapped by PVS that October, just as the 68 was being one-manned. *Geoff Rixon*

Left: Nowadays, Sundays see either side of Waterloo Bridge heaving with parked cars while their occupants go off to enjoy the West End, but on Sunday 1 August 1982 the only person who has turned out to watch Croydon's RM121 (VLT 121) gain the South Bank is a lone small boy. Only half a mile across the bridge is Aldwych, which would be the last London terminus this Routemaster would serve when removed from the 13 in October 2005. It had been withdrawn from Catford in June 1984 and spent the next decade at Cobham Bus Museum before a spell with Capital Citybus, which sold it back to London Transport (or Transport for London, as it became in 2000) during the short-lived final renaissance of the Routemaster. Since 2000 registered SSL 806, RM121 was on the brink of a new career as a tourist bus in Oxford in 2006 before the proprietor was obliged by the Traffic Commissioner to take this and his other three Marshall-refurbished RMs off the road after just three days, due to a licensing irregularity. *Geoff Rixon*

Route 52A
Converted from RM to crew M, summer 1986

Above: The 52A was introduced on the day of Westbourne Park garage's opening — 15 August 1981 — in order to give the 52's short-workings a more efficient objective than Ladbroke Grove and serve hitherto untapped streets. On 4 September 1982 the 52A was reallocated to Victoria and withdrawn on Sundays, and during mid-1986 crew Metrobuses began the conversion to doored bus operation prior to the date scheduled for the releasing of their conductors. The 52A was revamped in 1991 as new minibus route 70, which survives today. Here Victoria's RM2073 (ALM 73B) approaches Hyde Park Corner on 26 August 1985, by which time it had received its final body (B2010), with illuminated advertisement panel. Withdrawn in May 1986 and despatched to Kelvin Scottish, it was subsequently sold to Regal of Kirkintilloch, ultimately being scrapped by Wigley early in 1995. *Colin Brown*

Route 171
Converted from RM/crew T to OPO T, 25 October 1986

Right: Tram-replacement route 171 was operating between Forest Hill and Bruce Grove on the day RMs took over, 7 September 1968. Tottenham and New Cross shared the route, and that remained the state of affairs 13 years later, when each garage's participation was separated to form overlapping sections. However, the Sunday service continued to cover the entire length of the route and on 3 August 1985, by now provided only by New Cross, was converted to OPO T. On 1 February 1986 the Tottenham-operated Monday-Saturday section was separated entirely as new OPO route 171A, and the 171 fell back to Rosebery Avenue, Sadler's Wells. It was soon realised that this terminus was unsuitable, and on 21 June the 171 was restored as far north as Islington Green, the last act before permanent one-manning on 25 October with Titans, some of which were already in place. On 19 April 1980, plain-windowed RM600 (WLT 600), fresh from overhaul and newly assigned to New Cross, is on a short-working to Camberwell Green, close to Camberwell garage. It was withdrawn from Streatham in May 1988 and exported four years later to Japan. *Geoff Rixon*

Route 24
Converted from RML to OPO M/T, 25 October 1986

Left: The 24, despite serving many of the same London landmarks as the more famous route 11, always rather languished in the latter's shadow. Nevertheless, its usefulness is underscored by the extraordinary fact that not a single routeing change has been applied in over 90 years, although several generations of buses (and, more recently, operators) have come and gone. RMs, working from Chalk Farm, were introduced on 1 December 1963, only to be dislodged on 7 November 1965 by XA-class Leyland Atlanteans. This experiment concluded, the 24 was converted to RML operation on 12 June 1966, remaining thus for the next two decades — barring an unhappy interlude with DMs between 19 October 1975 and 22 April 1979. Only Victoria garage ever seriously tried to crack Chalk Farm's monopoly, on Saturdays between 24 January 1970 and 13 June 1972. On 12 January 1980 RML2473 (JJD 473D) has just swung around the Camden one-way system past Mornington Crescent station; this bus would serve until 2 July 2004, the last day of the 7 as a crew route, and now resides in Linz, Austria. *Geoff Rixon*

Right: On the same day but a little farther to the south, approaching Warren Street, is another Chalk Farm stalwart, RML2735 (SMK 735F). This was another bus to make its way eventually to Westbourne Park garage and come under the ægis of CentreWest; along with RML885 it became one of the post-LBL company's two showbuses, both of which were active on the last day of conductors on the 7. It has made more than a few guest appearances where approved on assorted last days and specials, the last of which was supporting a running day on the Heritage components of routes 9 and 15 on 17 September 2006. *Geoff Rixon*

Below right: One of the more noteworthy Routemasters to serve at Chalk Farm garage was RM1933 (ALD 933B), another of the four RMs treated to 1933-style livery to celebrate London Transport's Golden Jubilee in 1983. While more common on the 3 and 68, it is seen passing through Camden one day that August when the market (now a daily event) was not in session. Continuing at Chalk Farm until May 1986, RM1933 would go on to serve with Kelvin Scottish and two Stagecoach subsidiaries (Perth and Cumberland) before being brought back to the capital for the expansion of crew services undertaken in the first year of TfL. From June 2001 until mid-October 2005 it served on the 13 from Sovereign's Edgware depot, and a further lucky break saw it redeployed to Stagecoach East London and smartened up for use on the Heritage section of the 15 from 14 November 2005. *Geoff Rixon*

Route 52
Converted from RM to OPO M, 25 October 1986

Above: Compare Willesden's RM17 (VLT 17) with either of its fellow Golden Jubilee-celebrating RMs on pages 33, 57 and 67; there are subtle livery differences around the cab area. By the time of this shot, taken on 13 August 1983 at Willesden garage, the 52 had been RM-operated for more than 16 years, the type having displaced RTs from both Victoria and Willesden on 31 December 1966; on the same date the last Sunday projections beyond Mill Hill Broadway to Borehamwood were withdrawn. Victoria's allocation was transferred to Middle Row on 24 January 1970, and from 15 August 1981 Westbourne Park replaced Middle Row — but only on Sundays, the rest of its allocation being used to furnish new route 52A, as described on page 66. At the end of crew operation Willesden could field 19 RMs on the 52 before OPO Ms took over on 25 October 1986. RM17, repainted in February 1984 after the order to remove all manifestations of Golden Jubilee euphoria, was withdrawn in May 1985 and despatched to Clydeside Scottish (251); it later passed to Western Scottish (C11) but lost its registration in the process. Happily, the bus was acquired in 1995 by a Harwich-based preservationist, but the closest he could get to an appropriate registration for it was WLT 675, no longer needed by RM675, which had been scrapped in 1993. *Geoff Rixon*

Right: RM32 (VLT 32) swings out of the bus station into Grosvenor Gardens at the Victoria end of the 52 on 1 June 1980. Transferred from Stamford Brook the previous month, it would serve at Willesden until overhaul beckoned in April 1984. A variety of garages would make use of this bus as it was repeatedly withdrawn and reprieved, but the end finally came in May 1994 when it was taken out of service from Clapton, donating its registration to a Leyland Olympian before it went. In September 1997 it was sold to a buyer in Turkey. *Geoff Rixon*

Route 113
Converted from RM to OPO M, 25 October 1986

Above: The semi-motorway routeing of the 113 between Edgware and Childs Hill along Hendon Way would seem to have tempted an earlier OPO conversion than 25 October 1986, but once it joined up with the 13 it had to slog through treacle-slow traffic on its way to the West End and Oxford Circus. Operated solely by Hendon, it was converted from RT to RM on 1 September 1966, the peak vehicle requirement gradually declining from 22 buses to 16 two decades later, although RMLs had taken over on 28 February 1976. The new Brent Cross shopping centre, opened that year to immediate popularity, was soon allotted short-workings of the 113, which normally crossed the Staples Corner roundabout a few hundred yards to the east. Hendon's RML2663 (SMK 663F) sets off from the bus station on 2 May 1981; it would remain based in North London for the rest of its life, working from Finchley, the Borehamwood and Edgware depots of BTS/Sovereign and finally Tottenham before withdrawal on 3 September 2004, the infamous 'Black Friday'. *Colin Brown*

Right: A somewhat half-hearted attempt was made to one-man the 113's outer portion from 2 November 1985 by extending the 186 from Edgware to Brent Cross. The 113 was curtailed at the dubious traffic objective of Mill Hill, Apex Corner, which destination is clearly displayed on Hendon's RML2708 (SMK 708F) as it reposes at the route's Oxford Circus stand at John Prince's Street — still used today by the 113, which has been fully restored through to Edgware station. RML2708 also gravitated to Tottenham and was withdrawn from there in September 2004; it is now owned by an officer of the Routemaster Operators' & Owners' Association, who regularly brings it to events such as Cobham Bus Museum's open day. *Steve Smith collection*

Route 237
Converted from RML to crew M, winter 1986/1987

Above: It was a quirk of fate that transformed backwater RF service 237 into a crew-operated trunk route on 28 January 1978, swapping its role with that of the 117. Hounslow's RM1005 (5 CLT), destined to be the last Routemaster on the 13 (on 21 October 2005), is seen heading west through Chiswick on a short working to Lower Feltham on 12 October 1978. From that year, when Hounslow garage was given a portion of the 37 and a dozen RMLs, the longer Routemasters would oftentimes wander to the 237. Crew Ms would replace almost all of the RMs in time for the 237's conversion to OPO on 7 February 1987. *Geoff Rixon*

Left: The sleepy Sunbury terminus, right on the river's edge, was about as far physically and temperamentally from the hustle and bustle of Shepherd's Bush, the other end of the 237, as one could wish. The roads beyond Sunbury beyond the Greater London boundary to Chertsey were abandoned when the 237 took over the 117's role as a trunk route, and with the splitting in two of the 237 in 1996 the main effort of the route has shifted northeastwards again, now reaching only as far south as Hounslow Heath. This stand is nowadays used by single-deckers on route 235 but in October 1982 was host to RM2101 (ALM 101B), allocated to Hounslow. A high-profile deployment awaited this bus after its withdrawal from Wandsworth in March 1987, as it would form one of Southend Transport's much-admired fleet of Routemasters. After that operation had come to an end RM2101 would make its way abroad to eastern Germany, taking up a somewhat incongruous role as a playbus for the Weimar branch of McDonald's. *Geoff Rixon*

Route 149
Converted from RM to crew M, winter 1986/7

Left: Until 19 July 1961 the Hertford Road was the province of trolleybus route 649, but after that date 36 new RMs based at Edmonton inaugurated brand-new route 149, advancing beyond the 649's Liverpool Street terminus to Waterloo and Victoria; the northern terminus was Waltham Cross. Contraction at either end was the inevitable lot of the 149 as the decades rolled by, and at the end of crew operation it linked Enfield garage and Liverpool Street, with peak-hour-only runs to Waterloo. Vehicle policy had seen surprising twists: on 2 February 1974 both Edmonton and Stamford Hill (which had contributed on weekdays and Saturdays since 11 October 1961) received DMSs with their AFC (automatic fare collection) cabinets locked out of use; a year later purpose-built DMs took over. However, the unreliability of the Fleetlines led to the drive to restore Routemasters wherever possible, and the 149 duly became the new home of the superb RCL class of former Green Line coaches. Although downgraded to bus format by the removal of their twin headlights, platform doors and overhead luggage racks, the RCLs retained their thickly cushioned seats, ensuring a more comfortable ride. Seen at Victoria on 18 August 1980, Stamford Hill's RCL2218 (CUV 218C) would be withdrawn in March 1984, spending part of its retirement as a mobile family day centre before acquisition by the Nottingham Transport Heritage Centre. *Geoff Rixon*

Right: Policy changed, unfortunately, and the RCLs drifted away in ones and twos from 1982 until RCL2260 performed its last journey on 15 December 1984. Just coming up to Lower Edmonton (today known as Edmonton Green) on 27 March 1982 is one of the replacements, RM232 (VLT 232), freshly outshopped from Aldenham to Edmonton garage. An offside shot of this bus taken on the same day appears on the back cover, its subsequent career being detailed on page 2. *Geoff Rixon*

Left: Stamford Hill's contribution the 149 in the summer of 1981 was officially 15 RCLs, but on 28 July controllers saw fit to allow RM1681 (681 DYE) to stray from the 253, on which 38 RMs were deployed. Victoria Street, where the bus is pictured, is served today by considerably fewer buses, all of routes 29, 39, 70, 76, 134 and 149 having been removed from this thoroughfare during the Routemaster era. With the 149 long since curtailed to Waterloo (which objective was itself reached only at peak times), the route's replacement Metrobuses, released at the end of 1986 from Norwood and Croydon by incoming Ls, would not get to glimpse Victoria. By the turn of the year sufficient Ms had arrived at Enfield and Stamford Hill to allow most of the 149 to be doored once again in advance of OPO conversion on 7 February 1987. RM1681 lasted into 1992, training work (latterly with Westlink) becoming its lot in its final years before export to France. *Geoff Rixon*

EIGHT

Divide and Rule

PAINFUL death-throes seemed to be in the offing for the RM family in 1987. On 7 February the 30 and 74 lost their conductors; the 30 was cut back severely to lose both its Putney allocation and its service beyond West Brompton, Clapton garage taking on some more of the Titan surplus. The 74, worked by both Putney and Holloway, lost the Holloway share in favour of an increased Putney run-out with Ms. At Thornton Heath DMSs carried out the one-manning of the 109, while the 149 and 237 retained a mere handful of RMs to the end.

The 1986 batch of Ls was to be LBL's last volume order; instead of ordering new vehicles it made the difficult decision to save money by allowing tendering losses to furnish OPO conversions for the foreseeable future. To provide sufficient Ms for the 207's twice-deferred OPO conversion on 28 March, four routes had to be converted to LS operation. The 207's last day as a crew service, with RMLs lasting to the end at both Hanwell and Uxbridge, was attended by preserved RT3314.

For some years a backwater service despite its prestigiously low number, the 1 was propelled to prominence from 6 June upon its extension to Bromley Common and accompanying conversion from RM to OPO T at New Cross and Catford, with Bromley now joining in. At Leyton the 55 was one-manned for the second of an eventual three times, losing RMLs and its service beyond Tottenham Court Road to Titans and thus reintroducing double-deck OPO to the garage. A month later, on 11 July, routes 43 and 49 were converted to OPO, the 43 at Muswell Hill losing RMLs for Ms, and the 49's majority share passing from Merton to Streatham with a mix of Ms and Ls, with Shepherd's Bush using Ms. A change of heart on the Tower/Bank corridor from 6 June removed the 15A in favour of a split service on the 15, while that summer saw Upton Park's RMLs attempt to crack the tourist market with a Sunday-only 150 running between the Tower of London and Victoria. It lasted only three months, ceasing on 31 August.

The vehicle movements thrown up by the Harrow Buses programme, which substituted Harrow Weald's fleet of standard Ms for a motley collection of Volvo Ailsas, hired ex-Greater Manchester Fleetlines and leased Mk II Metrobuses, provided sufficient Ms to convert the 279 and 279A to OPO at Enfield, on 26 September, and the 16 and 16A at Cricklewood, on 21 November. Most controversially of all, on the latter date

the 253, at the time London's most heavily provisioned bus route, was one-manned despite several protests. Showbus RM83 led the final convoy of RMs on the last night, after which Stamford Hill replaced the route's RM/RML mix with Ms and Ash Grove took Ts to supplant its RMs.

If 1987 had been a tough year, worse was to follow in 1988. The 25 and 53, crew routes running nearly a hundred buses between them, fell to OPO on 16 January, their buses made available by the launch of the notorious Bexleybus network. Sixty Titans were drafted into Bow for the 25, while the unhappy closure of the recently refurbished Sidcup garage released enough Titans and Olympians to Plumstead and New Cross for the 53.

However, with the tipping-point clearly reached, second thoughts were entertained about further OPO conversions, and a moratorium was called. Saturday 5 November 1988 saw just two OPO conversions, both facilitated by the very high-profile tendering loss of the 24 to Grey-Green. Rather than imperil that route's operating garage, Chalk Farm, with closure, it was tasked to switch its Titans to the 29, Palmers Green receiving Ms in lieu of RMs and the Holloway and Wood Green shares coming off altogether. Holloway's shortfall was made up by one-manning the 135, an RM route introduced only on 21 November 1987 as a means of converting the northernmost section of the 137 to OPO.

With the activation of the pre-privatisation subsidiaries of LBL over the turn of 1988/9, planners had other things to worry about than the replacement of Routemasters, which, along with the rest of the London Buses fleet, now sprouted new unit fleetnames. By the end of the decade, after a period of neglect exacerbated by the closure of Aldenham Works in October 1986, some money was being invested in the Routemaster fleet as many were fitted with new Iveco or Cummins engines. The new 'tape-grey' fleet livery of 1988 had not altered the appearance of the class other than by a lick of grey paint over the dog rails, and a bit of pride was beginning to return to the buses — although not for the RMs working routes 28 and 31 out of Westbourne Park, which were taken away on 4 March (28) and 15 April (31) 1989 in favour of 70 distinctly unwelcome Mercedes-Benz minibuses, which were marketed under the title of Gold Arrow. These were the last OPO conversions of what had proved to be a very difficult decade.

Route 30
Converted from RM to OPO M/OPO T, 7 February 1987

Left: Plying between Hackney Wick and Roehampton (Earl Spencer), the 30 was a busy route that was quick to receive Routemasters once the trolleybuses had been replaced; Putney garage's contribution was converted on 1 June 1964, Hackney's following on 1 July, RTLs being replaced in both cases. The 30 required relatively little alteration, and in the following decade and a half the only change was the phasing-in of RMLs on Sundays. However, on 25 April 1981, consequent upon Hackney's closure and replacement by Ash Grove, the 30's southernmost end was re-routed via Putney Heath to reach Roehampton, swapping Dover House Road with the 74. On 4 September 1982 Ash Grove gave way to Clapton. In Jubilee Year (1983) the gold Routemaster, RM1983 (ALD 983B), was allocated to Clapton for a spell, being pictured in its home garage in September of that year, before the gold finish had had time to tarnish. Its last posting in gold was to Clapham, where it remained after repaint back into red livery. It was withdrawn in June 1986 upon the 37's one-manning, passing thereafter to Cumberland Motor Services. *Steve Smith collection*

Right: Bound for Hackney Wick, plain-windowed RM192 (VLT 192) pauses at Baker Street station on 15 June 1985 while working from Clapton garage. This would be its final allocation before withdrawal in June 1987, shortly before the first closure of the garage; it was subsequently exported to Sweden. *Colin Brown*

Below right: Putney's participation is represented by another plain-windowed Routemaster, RM185 (VLT 185), photographed during June 1986. Looking past its best, it would serve only six more months before sale to the breakers at PVS. After years of operating to Roehampton (Earl Spencer) the 30 was subjected in its final years of crew operation to considerable tinkering at its southern end, which began with the re-routing via Putney Heath in 1981. The inability of planners to make their minds up as to which estate in Roehampton should be served at weekends ended up with the route being taken out of the Alton East Estate at Bessborough Road and pointed instead to the Alton West Estate at Danebury Avenue. At the other end, an hour's journey away, the 30 was re-routed in Dalston via Hackney Downs station rather than Graham Road, while a final alteration in the south would see it forsake Roehampton altogether, being curtailed at Putney Heath (Green Man). When one-man buses were introduced Clapton garage was in flux between its existing Metrobuses and an incoming fleet of Titans, which would soon prevail. *Steve Smith collection*

Route 74
Converted from RM to OPO M, 7 February 1987

Above: Wednesday 18 July 1962 saw the first glimmering of Routemaster operation on the 74 when two Highgate-operated workings were added on weekdays; although withdrawn that winter they returned the following July, and on 7 November 1965 the Putney allocation went over to RM. Until 1966 it was paired with the 74A, which left the main route's path at Baker Street to terminate at Marylebone, while the 74B was another route in the family, reaching Hammersmith rather than Putney Heath (or Kingston Vale at peaks) and being withdrawn in 1978. Conversion to RML was implemented on 1 June 1967. Holloway joined Putney on 25 April 1981, from which date the 74 was diverted via the erstwhile 30 routeing to Roehampton, but on Sundays it followed its old course up Putney Hill to Putney Heath, and on 4 April 1984 the Roehampton terminus was standardised as Danebury Avenue. As if to address all this confusion — three routes ploughed much the same path from Putney into town — the 74

was cut back heavily on 3 August 1985, and its section beyond West Brompton was devolved to an extension of OPO route 264; the Putney allocation came off other than on Sundays. On 4 May 1980 a smart-looking RM1932 (ALD 932B), worked by Putney, speeds round a less congested Hyde Park Corner than we would see today. Withdrawn from Stamford Brook in July 1987, the bus was scrapped almost immediately. *Geoff Rixon*

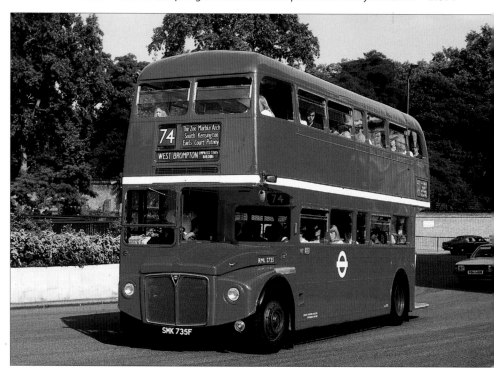

Right: Hyde Park Corner's west-facing quarter is the location on 10 July 1982 for Putney's RML2735 (SMK 735F), showing a destination that would become standard when the 74 was cut back on 3 August 1985. An earlier photograph of this bus appears on page 67. Neither the shortened 74 nor the extended 264 proved as viable in practice as they had looked on paper, and upon OPO conversion of the 74 on 7 February 1987 the 264 was swallowed up entirely. Yet in 2002 the 74 was split once again, its outer end becoming route 430. *Geoff Rixon*

Route 109
Converted from RM to OPO DMS, 7 February 1987

Above: A long and arduous trek from Central London to Croydon via the Brighton Road, the 109 was created out of tram routes 16 and 18 and employed so many RTs that it took until 1976 (and most of that year, at that) to amass enough RMs to convert the route. However, crew-operated doored buses were by then in vogue, and in August 1978 both the Brixton and Thornton Heath allocation succumbed to DMs. The Sunday service had been a different kettle of fish: with the 59 in charge of the north–south traffic only a vestigial service was retained to the Embankment loop, and this received two SMSs on 31 October 1970. DMSs followed, but the withdrawal of the 59 on 28 October 1978 reintroduced the 109 on Sundays as a crew service. Routemasters returned to the Brixton share on 15 August 1981 and to the (by now larger) Thornton Heath allocation on 4 September 1982, and all was as it had been, for a while longer at least. Just transferred from Fulwell on 15 August 1981, RM256 (VLT 256) reposes in the exit lane of Brixton garage, whose staff have removed the 'FW' coding but have yet to apply their own 'BN'. The bus was withdrawn from Croydon in August 1985 and scrapped by Wigley that November. *Geoff Rixon*

Left: Another Brixton bus, but an earlier arrival following outshopping from Aldenham in February 1980, RM187 (VLT 187) picks up in Streatham High Road, opposite Streatham garage. After another overhaul at the end of 1983 it worked from Battersea, Holloway and Tottenham before withdrawal in December 1986. It has certainly seen a varied life since then, working first for Western Scottish and then crossing the Atlantic to serve as an open-topper with the Beach Bus Company in Kittyhawk, North Carolina, where the Wright brothers made the first powered flight. In August 1997 it was bought by Double Deck Tours on the Canadian side of Niagara Falls. *Geoff Rixon*

Route 207
Converted from RML/crew M to OPO M, 28 March 1987

Right: Even today arguments rage about which form of transport is most suitable for the long and busy Uxbridge Road corridor. Tram route 7 begat trolleybus route 607, which gave way to the RM-operated 207 on 9 November 1960. Two periods of Routemaster operation characterised the following quarter-century, separated by an unhappy four years with crew-operated Fleetlines. This Ealing shot captures the changeover period from DM back to Routemaster operation commencing on 10 August 1980; in the same month we see RML2578 (JJD 578D), newly deployed to Hanwell garage, being pursued by DM1819 (GHM 819N), itself just a couple of weeks away from transfer from Hanwell to a more sympathetic home at Walthamstow. The Fleetline emigrated to Hong Kong in 1982, while RML2578 survived until 22 July 2005, finishing its days on the 14. In the same year the 207, shorn of its western half beyond Hayes End, succumbed to articulated buses — about as far as one could get from the prestige and comfort of trolleybuses or RMLs. *Geoff Rixon*

Left: During the second period of Routemaster operation on the 207 a mix of lengths endured until sufficient RMLs could be found to furnish the 51 workings required at the time. RM1544 (544 CLT) is seen in Ealing on 20 August 1980, 10 days into a new posting at Hanwell garage. A contract overhaul by Eastern Coach Works of Lowestoft early in 1984 would fail to save it from the scrapyard three years later. *Geoff Rixon*

Right: The conversion back to Routemaster operation of the 207 was made possible by London Transport's reacquisition from London Country of green RMLs and RCLs. RML2451 (JJD 451D) had last worked from Hemel Hempstead and prior to its overhaul was used as a trainer from North Street. Freshly allocated to Hanwell, it is seen in August 1980 at Ealing Common. It would be one of the Scania-engined Routemasters last used on the 8 from Bow but was withdrawn in April 2004 for use by one of Stagecoach's other subsidiaries. While in store at Carlisle it was deluged by floodwaters on 8 January 2005 but was thankfully repaired and awaits further deployment. *Geoff Rixon*

Route 15A
Withdrawn, 6 June 1987

Right: The Bank service provided by the 15 on its way from East End to West End fell out of favour with London Transport's planners, who observed that the City was virtually deserted at weekends, leaving the 15's large number of buses under-utilised. From 18 May 1985 the axis was switched to the Tower of London corridor, a late change of plan renumbering the 23 as the 15 and the rump Bank service of the 15 to 15A. What good the copious on-bus advertising and yellow-accented livery sported by Upton Park's sizeable fleet of RMLs may have accomplished is debatable, as the 15A was withdrawn on 6 June 1987 and its routeing swallowed up by the main 15, the 'VIA BANK' intermediate blinds and canopy blinds being retained. It seemed that the planners could not make their minds up: 18 months later a separate Bank service reappeared as the 15B, but less than two years after that the Bank leg was withdrawn altogether, the 25 being left to cope on its own. Working from Upton Park, RML2652 (NML 652E) makes the right turn out of Elgin Crescent into Ladbroke Grove In April 1987; it last saw service on the 6 and 98 at Willesden in March 2004. *Steve Smith collection*

Route 1
Converted from RM to OPO T/OPO L, 6 June 1987

Left: Despite its prestige number the 1 has always been something of a Cinderella route, rising and falling on the whims of planners. Conversion to RM would not come until 1975 (26 January at New Cross, 23 February at Catford), though Saturdays had seen RMs at New Cross since 1970. At the time the 1 ran between Oxford Circus and Catford garage, with a unique section along Southwark Park Road in Bermondsey; on weekdays it continued at either end to Marylebone and Bromley garage respectively. No service operated on Sundays until 31 October 1981 and again between 20 April 1984 and 2 November 1985 when the 1A ran. Catford garage was the 1's southeastern terminus from 28 October 1978, but 2 November 1985 saw the route diverted to Greenwich and the Catford allocation withdrawn (other than the OPO service on Sundays, introduced on this date in place of the 1A). In this 7 June 1980 view, RM1806 (806 DYE) passes a DMS outside Catford garage; Fleetlines would never trouble the 1, but Titans would take the route into OPO. RM1806 would not live to see that day, being withdrawn from Streatham in July 1984 and scrapped by PVS early in 1986. *Geoff Rixon*

Left: Seen at Waterloo on 16 April 1983 is RM1113 (113 CLT), allocated to New Cross. This would be the last garage to host this Routemaster, which was withdrawn in April 1986 and scrapped that October. One-manning saw the 1 regain Bromley garage as a terminus, but only four years later it was cut down even further, falling back all the way to Surrey Docks. The Southwark Park Road portion remains the 1's core section and is once again served by this route alone. *Geoff Rixon*

Route 55
Converted from RML to OPO T, 6 June 1987

Right: The 55 is an extremely rare example of a route that was converted from OPO back to crew; only two others were ever treated this way. Extraordinarily, in 2001 the 55 would regain conductors for a second time, though not with Routemasters; that was for the first occasion on 31 January 1981, when 20 RMs replaced an equivalent number of DMSs from Leyton garage. RM11 (VLT 11) was allocated there that March following overhaul, and in this view on 27 April demonstrates (albeit with the bonnet up) the revised role of the 55, which was an extension to Victoria in lieu of Waterloo. The other terminus was Walthamstow Central, but that too was to be altered, the route being diverted to Whipps Cross on 26 February 1983. *Geoff Rixon*

Below: Another view of RM11, this time rounding Hyde Park Corner on 15 August 1981, allows us to note that in less than four months the vehicle has become a showbus, with full-depth radiator grille, cream cantrail band, chrome headlight rings and, unusually, non-underlined LONDON TRANSPORT fleetnames. It would remain at Leyton until December 1986, when it was withdrawn and sold to PVS for scrap. *Geoff Rixon*

Route 43
Converted from RML to OPO M, 11 July 1987

Above: The 43 made most of its money from commuters joining and leaving the Northern Line at Highgate before heading into the City and London Bridge via Archway, the Holloway Road and Old Street; there was no Sunday service. RMs took over at Muswell Hill on 21 June 1963, to be replaced by RMLs on 16 January 1971, but the 43 was a route chosen for DMs from 26 January 1975. Second thoughts brought back RMs on 4 September 1982. On 23 April 1983 a Finchley allocation was introduced, and on 28 July 1984 that garage's relief journeys were livened up, continuing west from Friern Barnet to North Finchley. Caught in repose under the windswept canopy of London Bridge station on 1 October 1982, RM443 (WLT 443) would be withdrawn from Stockwell in July 1985 and scrapped by PVS the following month. *Steve Smith collection*

Right: The last act of the 43 as a crew route was its conversion from RM to RML on 21 June 1986, the replacements all coming from Finchley. Heading for London Bridge station, RML2353 (CUV 353C) is seen in City Road shortly after the changeover. It would go on to Shepherd's Bush, there to spend the rest of its service days until withdrawal in January 2004.
Steve Smith collection

Route 49
Converted from RM to OPO M/OPO L, 11 July 1987

Above: Traditionally operating between Shepherd's Bush and Crystal Palace, the 49 lost the section south of Streatham garage from 15 May 1971, the day its new fleet of RMs was transferred into Streatham and Merton. A Sunday projection at the other end to Harlesden was removed after 28 October 1978. This time it is the turn of RM1441 (441 CLT) to get a two-picture special, celebrating its status as Streatham garage's showbus; a difference from the usual treatment is the silver radiator grille. Here it passes St Leonard's Church in Streatham on 17 August 1981. *Geoff Rixon*

Left: In the same month RM1441 is seen a little further south, having made the sharp right-hand turn into Streatham High Road to pass its home garage. It would be withdrawn in November 1983 and scrapped almost immediately by C. F. Booth of Rotherham, too early to see the Streatham allocation withdrawn so that the garage could be rebuilt. This process lasted from 27 October 1984 until 7 February 1987, when a Streatham RM allocation was once again introduced; in the interim part of the 49 had been given to Shepherd's Bush. OPO ensued with three types: Ms from Shepherds Bush and Streatham, Ls also from Streatham and DMSs from Merton, which garage renewed its involvement on Sundays. *Geoff Rixon*

Route 150
Sunday-only tourist route withdrawn, 31 August 1987

Left: In 2007 one can find a dedicated tourist route centred on the Tower of London, but during the summer of 1987 Upton Park garage had the same idea, detaching a couple of RMLs from the 15 to perform a service linking the Tower and Victoria. The 150, however, was not a success and was withdrawn on 31 August after just three months of operation. Espied from atop Temple station on 31 May 1987, showbus RML2760 (SMK 760F) looks uncomfortable with an extra yellow band that sits unhappily alongside traditional gold fleetnames. This last of the Routemasters remained at Upton Park, seeing out the 15's Routemasters on 29 August 2003 and then doing the same at Bow for the 8 on 4 June 2004. *John Parkin*

Route 279
Converted from RM/crew M to OPO M, 26 September 1987

Right: Replacing trolleybus route 679 on 26 April 1961, the 279 operated from Smithfield to Waltham Cross; over the next decade sections were gradually projected beyond the Greater London boundary to Hammond Street, deep in Hertfordshire. Edmonton inaugurated the 279 but was joined on 24 January 1970 by Enfield. An early attempt to separate the Hammond Street section (as the 283) lasted only from 28 October 1978 to 27 September 1980, its abandonment leading to the anomaly of crew buses serving this rural Hertfordshire outpost well into the 1980s. Similarly the Sunday service was split in half and the town section one-manned as DMS route 279A, although on 28 October 1978 this was revamped as a crew service to Liverpool Street to serve the markets. On 3 August 1985 the Hammond Street service disappeared for good, transferred to the 259, and Edmonton's closure on 1 February 1986 left Enfield in sole charge. Here Enfield's RM971 (WLT 971) heads through Edmonton on a sunny 27 March 1982; it would be one of the first withdrawals six months later. Vic Berry was awarded the contract to break up this bus and a hundred others at Aldenham. *Geoff Rixon*

Route 279A
Converted from RM/crew M to OPO M, 26 September 1987

Left: Routes 43, 243 and 279 all sprouted Sunday variants with the specific task of serving the Sunday markets within reach of Liverpool Street. Having run with DMSs since 10 March 1973 as an adjunct to the 259, the 279A was revised on 28 October 1978 to become a Sunday service to the 279 proper, shared between Enfield and Edmonton and extended to Waltham Cross. Such was the state of affairs in February 1982, when Edmonton's RM287 (VLT 287) was captured heading south through Lower Edmonton. This garage's involvement ceased with its closure from 1 February 1986, and OPO conversion was effected on 26 September 1987 with Enfield Ms. The Liverpool Street bifurcation was ended on 1 February 1992 by the rather drastic expedient of axing the entire 279 service south of Holloway, but the market service was not replaced (and no longer exists on the 43 or 243 either). RM287 was withdrawn from Putney in January 1987 and scrapped in March of that year. *Geoff Rixon*

Route 16
Converted from RML/crew M to OPO M, 21 November 1987

Left: New Year's Day 1963 saw 54 RMs take over the 16, at the time an arrow-straight route from Victoria up the Edgware Road as far as Cricklewood, the operating garage, after which it took a westerly course to Sudbury Town station via Neasden. This last named became the terminus on 13 January 1970, when new route 245 took over the Sudbury service, while crew-operated Fleetlines were phased in during December 1973 — first DMSs and then, nearly a year later, DMs. Routemasters, this time RMLs, returned on 25 May 1980, but in the interim half the service had been separated (as the 16A) to provide a link to the new Brent Cross shopping centre. Not far from here is the junction of the North Circular Road with the beginning of the M1, under which RML2309 (CUV 309C) is passing on 24 July 1980. This former Country Area bus, which last worked at Northfleet before being bought back by London Transport, would last until 2 July 2004, when the 7 from Westbourne Park was one-manned, and is now owned by two preservationists from Sheffield. *Geoff Rixon*

Below: RML2333 (CUV 333C) was another of its type rescued from London Country Bus Services and was deployed after overhaul to Cricklewood for the 16 and 16A. Photographed on 17 April 1981, it had almost completed one of the 16's southbound journeys to Victoria, being seen passing the Hilton Hotel on Park Lane and with just Hyde Park Corner to negotiate. This bus would reach Brixton garage in time to see off the last regular route (159) but would be stood down before the end. *Geoff Rixon*

Above: Swinging out of Victoria bus station on 29 July 1983 is RML2327 (CUV 327C), another former Country Area / LCBS Routemaster. On the pillar just ahead of the platform can be seen a sticker denoting that this bus and its operating garage, Cricklewood, were the responsibility of Cardinal District. This represented an early attempt to divide London's buses into more manageable sections and was subject to amendment as requirements changed; Cricklewood had initially been part of Watling District. The district system would lead to the antecedents of the post-LBL companies we know today. RML2327 finished at Camberwell late in 2003 and was sold to the Halifax Joint Committee for preservation. *Geoff Rixon*

Route 16A
Converted from RML/crew M to OPO M, 21 November 1987

Right: The 16A was introduced on 31 January 1976 to serve the new Brent Cross shopping centre, but not until 25 May 1980 were its DMs (and five crew-operated prototype Metrobuses) replaced by RMLs. Further variety was ensured by RMs straying from other Cricklewood routes, as RM517 (WLT 517) is doing here at a rainy Victoria bus station on 31 May 1980. On 25 April 1981 the 16A would be withdrawn from Victoria and re-routed at Marble Arch down Oxford Street to Oxford Circus. Norbiton would be the final garage of this bus; it was withdrawn in April 1985 and scrapped by Rollinson of Carlton. *Geoff Rixon*

Route 253
Converted from RM to OPO M/OPO T, 21 November 1987

Right: It was natural that the 253, one of the most heavily-provisioned trolleybus-replacement routes, should come to be worked by more garages than a less busy route; in its Routemaster era between introduction on 1 February 1961 and OPO conversion on 21 November 1987 it saw participation at various times by Highgate (Holloway), Edmonton, Stamford Hill, Clapton, Dalston and Ash Grove. Only in the late 1980s did the 253's peak vehicle requirement slip below 50 buses. In June 1980 RM1700 (700 DYE) was one of the 22 RMs of Stamford Hill's allocation, in comparison with Clapton's 15 and Dalston's 16; it is pictured rounding Mornington Crescent station on its way to Warren Street, a terminus since replaced by Euston. Although re-registered KGJ 167A in 1992, RM1700 remained in service until December 1997, finishing at Holloway in the all-red livery of MTL London, whose route 139 was one-manned on 28 March 1998. It was scrapped on site and written off by February 1998. *Geoff Rixon*

Above: Before its reawakening as Croydon's showbus (see page 41), RM1000 (100 BXL) was just another standard Routemaster. When sighted at Mornington Crescent in April 1980 it was allocated to Clapton and had mismatched front wings, the nearside example originating on a much newer RML. Overhaul a few months later would take it to Croydon. *Geoff Rixon*

Route 25
**Converted from RM to OPO T,
16 January 1988**

Right: Ploughing an arrow-straight path for 15 miles from Becontree Heath to Bond Street before making the left turn towards Green Park and Victoria, the 25 was (and remains) a key trunk route. When conversion from RT to RM took place on 8 January 1972 Bow had 32 workings and West Ham 19, somewhat down from the 80-plus workings of two decades previously, but the Victoria Line's opening had taken away a goodly proportion of its custom. On 4 September 1982 the route was withdrawn between Ilford and Becontree Heath, replaced over that section by new route 225 (see page 29). The Bow/West Ham partnership would endure, but from 2 November 1985 West Ham would have only the Sunday operation, which had been converted to OPO T eight months earlier, paving the way for the rest. Passing Debenham's in Oxford Street on its long haul to Ilford one day in June 1981 is Bow's RM2092 (ALM 92B). This bus would remain at Bow until the 25's OPO conversion and then leave these shores for a career in Sri Lanka. *Geoff Rixon*

Below: The Royal Wedding of Prince Charles and Lady Diana Spencer took place on 29 July 1981 at St Paul's Cathedral. London Transport sent its best wishes through the means of applying a silver 'parcel ribbon' livery to eight RMs after trials with RM490. Bow's representative, allocated to the 25, was RM561 (WLT 561), pictured crossing Oxford Circus on 15 June 1981. The seven buses performed a tour over the procession route on the day before the wedding and were then present at the fireworks display. Sadly, the marriage was not to last, and neither was RM561, which was withdrawn from Edmonton in March 1985 and scrapped by PVS two months later. By the time of Prince Charles's second wedding, in 2005, there was no longer a London Transport around to celebrate it. *Geoff Rixon*

Route 53
Converted from RM to OPO L/OPO T, 16 January 1988

Right: Another long and important trunk route, the 53 operated from Camden Town in a southeasterly direction, terminating at Plumstead Common. RMs appeared in 1967, the Plumstead (AM) allocation going over on 1 July and New Cross following suit on 1 September. In 1969 the New Cross share was increased, and on 24 January 1970 Plumstead withdrew. Saturday 8 January 1977 saw the 53 converted to doored buses — but MDs rather than DMs. Although better-performing than the Fleetline, the Metropolitans gave way to returning RMs on 31 October 1981. A surprising extension on 27 October 1984 took the 53 to Parliament Hill Fields over the 3, and on 3 August 1985 the new Plumstead (PD) garage received its first allocation of RMs to allow conductors to remain employed following the one-manning of the 180. During 1981 New Cross was allotted one of the seven Royal Wedding-liveried Routemasters, RM607 (WLT 607), which is seen at Waterloo Place in July. Like Bow counterpart RM561 it did not survive, coming off service in May 1984 and being scrapped in August by Wigley. *Geoff Rixon*

Right: On 27 March 1982 a slightly grubby-looking RM21 (VLT 21) of New Cross garage demonstrates an important change to the traffic arrangements made to Parliament Square for a spell during the 1980s; rather than battle round all four corners of the square into Whitehall northbound buses were given a contra-flow right-hand-turn lane, which RM21 is about to use. Unfortunately this feature has since been abandoned. RM21's last overhaul in June 1980 gave it a Leyland engine, which put it higher up the list for withdrawal than the majority of AEC-engined RMs; this duly took place in July 1984, the bus being broken up a month later at Wigley's scrapyard. *Geoff Rixon*

Right: With the opening of the new Plumstead garage on 31 October 1981, the 53's occasional meal-relief projections from Plumstead Common were re-routed to this location rather than the old Plumstead garage, which had stood to the east. New Cross's RM691 (WLT 691) displays the appropriate blinds as it passes along Whitehall on 6 May 1985. It was transferred to Holloway that December and served another year there before withdrawal in February 1986 and sale to PVS. *Colin Brown*

Route 29
Converted from RM to OPO M, 5 November 1988

Above: The OPO conversion of the 29 demonstrated that by 1988 not even the most major trunk routes were immune to cost-cutting. When RMs arrived on 7 September 1968 (22 from Holloway and 24 from Wood Green) the 29 still penetrated beyond Southgate to Cockfosters during the peaks and even as far as South Mimms on Sunday afternoons; retrenchment in 1971 saw those projections cut back. On 14 December 1975 the 29 was converted experimentally to DM operation. The results having proved unsatisfactory, renaissance came on 19 March 1977 with the route's reversion to RM and diversion to Enfield Town; Palmers Green now joined Holloway and Wood Green. Growth was such that the new terminus was often packed with 29s, three of which — RMs 384 (WLT 384), 372 (WLT 372) and 2073 (ALM 73B) — are seen posing on 23 January 1982. They were withdrawn in November 1985, April 1991 and May 1986 respectively, none escaping the breakers. *Geoff Rixon*

Above: On 24 May 1981 Palmers Green's RM1428 (428 CLT) is on its way down Victoria Street. It was withdrawn from Holloway garage in February 1994 and allocated to the reserve then being formed; however, it would not see further service in the capital, and its present whereabouts are unknown. *Geoff Rixon*

Right: As the 1980s progressed the sciences of marketing and advertising gained ground — but when have London's classic buses really needed any help drawing attention to themselves? Appearing first on the 23 in 1984, route branding soon degenerated to the application of rather brash yellow posters accompanying yellow cantrail bands and blind lettering. Such was the fate of Palmers Green's RM476 (WLT 476), coming round Parliament Square in May 1987. Route branding also hindered flexibility where a garage ran more than one RM-operated route, but the 29 was by now Palmers Green's only such service. RM476 was withdrawn in October 1988, just before OPO conversion of the 29, and scrapped by Wigley. *Geoff Rixon*

Route 135
Converted from RM to OPO M, 5 November 1988

Left: The second route 135 in this account was a localisation of the 137's northern-most section to Archway introduced on 21 November 1987, allowing that service to fall back to Oxford Circus. The 135 was Holloway-operated with nine RMs like RM2190 (CUV 190C), reposing at Archway on 21 October 1988. This was one of a sizeable number of buses at North London garages to receive blinds in all-upper-case lettering, something not seen for over two decades. With the advent of Metrobuses on 5 November crew operation on the 135 was to last just short of a year. The route was withdrawn in 2000 without direct replacement other than augmentations to parallel services. RM2190 remained at Holloway until April 1989 and was later sold for scrap. *Steve Smith collection*

Route 28
Converted from RM to OPO MA, 4 March 1989

Above: History will tell whether the conversion of two busy Routemaster services to van-based minibuses was a sensible thing, especially as both have recently reverted to double-deck operation. The 28 had been converted from RT to RM on 18 April 1970, although the Middle Row allocation had been thus on Sundays since 1964. Wandsworth was the other garage in charge and withdrew only upon closure on 11 July 1987, on which date the Sunday service was converted to OPO. In the meantime 15 August 1981 had seen Middle Row's allocation moved to Westbourne Park with the same X code, but in the 18 years of RM operation the total peak vehicle requirement dwindled steadily, from 31 to 20 buses. At Golders Green on 28 July 1984 any passenger attempting to board what looks like an offside set of stairs on Wandsworth's RM960 (WLT 960) would be in for a rude shock, this actually being a surprisingly authentic-looking L-shaped advertisement promoting Colt 45 lager. Withdrawn from Wood Green garage in March 1987, the bus subsequently joined the Clydeside Scottish fleet and is now preserved. *Colin Brown*

Route 31
Converted from RM to OPO MA, 15 April 1989

Above: The second route to be re-branded as 'Gold Arrow' with its rattly Mercedes-Benz minibuses, the 31 had also enjoyed nearly two decades with RMs, its allocation at Battersea and Chalk Farm being converted thus on 17 June 1972, although, as with the 28, weekend services had been in the hands of Routemasters prior to the full conversion from RT. On 4 September 1982 both garages withdrew in favour of a sole Westbourne Park allocation; this was joined by Holloway on weekdays between 7 February and 21 November 1987, but on the latter date the inevitable Sunday OPO conversion was accomplished by moving the 31 into Chalk Farm on that day of the week, and such was the situation on 15 April 1989, when the 31's 16 RMs (five from Holloway, 11 from Westbourne Park) were replaced by 25 MAs. Chalk Farm's RM1190 (190 CLT) is seen at Notting Hill Gate a decade earlier, in October 1979. One of the earliest withdrawals, in September 1982, it last worked from Ash Grove and was cut up at Aldenham by Vic Berry of Leicester. *Geoff Rixon*

Left: From time to time RMLs would get out on the 31, Westbourne Park, Chalk Farm and Holloway garages all allowing their longer Routemasters to wander from their allocated routes. On 29 July 1988 Westbourne Park's RML2553 (JJD 553D) is seen in Pembridge Villas sporting a fresh new coat of red paint. Also of interest is the revised London Buses roundel introduced the previous year, which, while a little garish for the sides of London buses, would last only until LBL's subsidiaries were privatised in 1994. RML2553 remained at Westbourne Park for the rest of its life, leaving service in November 2003 and passing to First Glasgow. *Steve Smith collection*

The Road to Requiem

BY the 1990s it was clear that the Routemaster family had again cheated death, despite having been depleted in numbers by 75% since the autumn of 1982. As the decade progressed, LSs, DMSs and then Ts took their place as withdrawal candidates, and OPO conversions numbered just eight routes in the whole decade.

From 23 November 1991 route X15 gained Titans to replace the superbly treated RMCs at Upton Park. The final stage of retrenchment to the once-mighty 36B at Catford garage brought crew Ts just before its one-manning on 14 March 1992, making Selkent the first all-OPO LBL subsidiary; prior to that the 36 group had been simplified with the withdrawal of the peak-hour-only 36A on 27 April 1991. Route 15B, which had been commissioned from 4 March 1989 to differentiate the Bank routeing once again, was reconfigured on 18 July 1992 to one-man the end of the 15 east of Canning Town, taking brand-new Scanias for its trouble. Years of decline on the 88, aggravated by the loss of its western end and Shepherd's Bush share to new route 94 in 1990, were capped with the arrival of Ms in time for its OPO conversion on 15 August 1992. Brand-new DAF DB250/Optare Spectras (SPs) carried out the one-manning of the 3 at Camberwell on 4 January 1993; on 27 February that year the 2B, Norwood garage's last crew route, was renumbered plain 2, which lost its RMLs for OPO Ms and Ls on 29 January 1994. Finally the 139, introduced as the 159's new northern localisation in 1992, was fair game for the latest low-floor single-deckers, Dennis Dart SLFs, which took over on 28 March 1998.

Not long after the mass re-engining came the refurbishment programme of 1992-4, a £10 million exercise awarded to Mainline (South Yorkshire Transport) at Rotherham and TBP Holdings of West Bromwich, with LBL's Leaside Buses subsidiary treating its own vehicles. This saw the RML fleet comprehensively rewired, repanelled and reupholstered for 10 years' further service. Later in the decade Scania engines replaced many of the Ivecos, and as 2000 opened, a second generation of Cummins engine was unveiled, accompanied by a new transmission system manufactured by Allison.

Despite this admirable effort securing London's heritage and image into the 21st century, the axe finally fell on London Transport as a bus operator in 1994, when its 10 surviving subsidiaries (London Forest having been disbanded in November 1991) were sold to the private sector. Out went London Buses, and up stepped London Central, London General, London United, CentreWest (its Routemasters branded Gold Arrow), Metroline, MTL London Northern, Cowie Leaside, Cowie South London, Stagecoach East London and Routemaster-less Stagecoach Selkent. All developed subtle variations on London's traditional red livery, but adding to the variety were the RMLs hired to Kentish Bus and BTS, each of which had won a tender in 1993.

The story from this point in time to the final end of London Routemaster operation (Heritage routes excepted) is related in the authors' earlier volume *Routemaster Requiem*, published by Ian Allan in 2005.

Route 36A
Withdrawn, 27 April 1991

Left: On 14 January 1963 RMs replaced Rye Lane-based RTLs on the 36A, at that time operating Mondays-Saturdays between West Kilburn and Brockley Rise. Peckham took over on 22 March 1969 and remained in sole charge throughout the life of the route; however, the 36A became the familiar peak-hour-only service on 16 January 1971. MDs were in charge between 28 January 1976 and 17 February 1980, during which time the route was curtailed from the southeast at Victoria. A service as far as Paddington was restored briefly, but the route was held in little regard by the planners and was withdrawn on 27 April 1991 without replacement. RM1174 (174 CLT), its running-number-holders in the lowered position, indicating a BUSCO-equipped vehicle, is seen at Paddington on 19 May 1987. This bus would last until November 2004 (albeit latterly registered JSJ 797) and following withdrawal from Camberwell garage now resides in Essex.
Steve Smith collection

Route X15
Converted from RMC to OPO T, 23 November 1991

Right: Introduced on Monday 6 March 1989, new route X15 used seven superbly-reconditioned RMCs from Upton Park, operating a peak-hour 'with the flow' service between the revitalising Beckton area and Aldwych. It was extended two weeks later to Oxford Circus (inbound), the outbound evening peak journeys being back-projected to start at Trafalgar Square. The RMCs were sufficiently popular for three (RMCs 1456, 1461 and 1485) to be retained by Upton Park following the X15's one-manning, the trio thereafter seeing regular use on the 15 all the way to the end of Routemasters on that route on 29 August 2003. RMC1461 (461 CLT) operated in Green Line livery in later years and is preserved thus at Cobham Bus Museum. In the summer of 1989, which year saw *EAST LONDON* unit logos introduced to join the revised roundel of two years earlier, it is seen calling at Aldgate, with Titan T471 endeavouring to overtake. *Geoff Rixon*

Route 36B
Converted from RM to crew T, winter 1991/2

Right: The story of the 36B is truly one of rise and fall. By the time of the conversion of this tram-replacement route (originally numbered 69) to Leyland-engined RM on 15 January 1963 it had assumed the senior role in the trio of routes that also encompassed the 36 and 36A. However, all three routes were restocked in 1976 with Scania/MCW Metropolitans of the MD class. Doored crew operation fell quickly out of favour, and by 17 February 1980 a full complement of RMs was restored. RM14 (VLT 14) was assigned to Peckham in March 1980 following overhaul and is seen in Camberwell on 19 April. In 1983 the 36 group evaluated the BUSCO system of radio equipment; Catford received an allocation on the 36B on 2 November 1985. Still, rationalisation loomed. From 27 April 1991 the 36B was withdrawn west of Victoria and the 36 gained the ascendancy, the 36A being withdrawn outright. Incoming Titans prepared the 36B for OPO, which followed on 14 March 1992. Since 12 March 1994 the route has been known as 136 and runs no further west than Peckham. The main 36 survived to become London's seventh-last crew route; RM14 was withdrawn with accident damage in February 1994 while in showbus condition at Camberwell but (as OYM 424A) survives to this day. *Geoff Rixon*

Route 15B
Converted from RML to OPO S, 18 July 1992

Right: The 15B was introduced on 4 March 1989 to give the Bank section of the 15 a separate identity again but did not run at weekends or at all west of Oxford Circus. On 6 October 1990 it was withdrawn between Upton Park garage and East Ham and reduced to peak-only. Fifteen RMLs were allocated, one of which, RML2686 (SMK 686F), is pictured crossing Aldwych in May 1989; the route branding is now more sedate by this time, following a 'Bus It!' theme, while *EAST LONDON* unit fleetnames underscore the beginnings of more permanent division. Since 1999 the 15B has been known as 115 and does not serve Bank at all. Much of RML2686's last decade was spent in BTS (later Sovereign) poppy red on route 13; displaced by a Marshall-refurbished RM, it passed to Tottenham for the 73, finishing service on 3 September 2004. *Steve Smith collection*

Route 88
Converted from RM/crew M to OPO M, 15 August 1992

Above: For many years a long '7'-shaped route linking Acton Green and Mitcham, the 88 was shared by Shepherd's Bush and Stockwell when 48 RMs took over on 10 July 1965. Upgrading to RML followed on 24 January 1970, whereafter little ensued until the inevitable retrenchment of the 1980s. On 5 April 1980 Stockwell's RML2265 (CUV 265C) rounds Marble Arch; for some reason the bracket where the numberplate would normally be affixed under the radiator grille is not present, the plate being fastened untidily to the grille instead. Sunday OPO, with DMSs from Stockwell and Ms from Shepherd's Bush, was introduced on 21 November 1987, which date also saw the 88 withdrawn between Tooting and Mitcham. On 28 April 1990 it fell back further, to Clapham Common, and worse was to come on 22 September of that year, when the western end was hived off into new Shepherd's Bush-operated route 94, Stockwell garage now assuming sole responsibility for the surviving rump. The 88's Central London terminus became Marble Arch but was further retracted to Oxford Circus upon OPO conversion on 15 August 1992. Just prior to this date the long-established RMLs had been replaced by RMs and then by crew Ms. RML2265 finished at Tottenham, working on the 73's last day as a crew route on 3 September 2004, and was bought by a preservationist in Middlesbrough. *Geoff Rixon*

Left: On 25 April 1981 a Merton allocation was introduced on the 88 on Sundays only, the route being extended from Mitcham via Phipps Bridge Estate (on weekdays the preserve of the 200) to reach that garage. The most unusual blinds for that working, with the qualifier displayed before the destination, are displayed by Merton's RM2018 (ALM 18B), passing what was then known as the Ministry of Agriculture, Fisheries and Food (now DEFRA) in Whitehall on 27 August 1984. The Merton Sunday share was withdrawn on 1 February 1986, but 88s continued to call at the garage until the route was pulled back from the area. RM2018 was withdrawn from Merton in August 1986 and exported to Japan. *Colin Brown*

Route 3
Converted from RM/crew T to OPO SP, 4 January 1993

Above: When Chalk Farm and Norwood took RMs for the 3 on 1 October 1964, the route was running between Crystal Palace and Camden Town. The entire service north of Oxford Circus was swept away on 4 April 1987, but the core route still required 19 RMs. In the interim both Chalk Farm and Norwood had ceded their participation to Camberwell alone; two other garages to have had brief flirtations with the 3 were Stockwell (1981/2) and Walworth (1984/5), while vehicle variations from the norm had seen RMLs and, later, DMs working from Chalk Farm at weekends. Camberwell's RM2078 (ALM 78B) rests at Parliament Hill Fields in August 1984, shadowed by potential competition in the form of Holloway-based Metrobus M1032. However, at that time the preferred OPO double-decker of Camberwell garage was the Titan, sizeable numbers of which were transferred in at the end of 1992 to prepare the 3 while the intended DAF DB250/Optare Spectras were run in on the 40. OPO conversion ensued on 4 January 1993, but Routemasters made return appearances for two days of the following week when the SPs took it upon themselves to fail *en masse.* After withdrawal from Willesden in August 1993 RM2078 was kept back for the Reserve fleet, patiently waiting until Shepherd's Bush took it on in 1997 to fill a need on the 9 and 94. In August 2004 it was sold to two individuals in Hampton. *Steve Smith collection*

Left: Comprehensive refurbishment makes Whitehall unrecognisable during November 1988 as Camberwell's RM2128 (CUV 128C) passes through on the 3. The 'ultimate' blinds are in the rather unattractive Helvetica font used for a couple of years during the mid-1980s when Aldenham was being run down and suppliers were not provided with the standard Johnston typescript. RM2128 had a long career, circumstances stranding it south of the river; working out of New Cross (route 36) and Stockwell (11) before being reallocated back to Camberwell for the 12, it would spend its dying days at New Cross. It ran for the final time on 28 January 2005 on the 36's last day with Routemasters and now resides in Lincolnshire. *Steve Smith collection*

Route 2B
Withdrawn (renumbered 2), 27 February 1993

Above: The 2B was another suffixed afterthought to assume the main role in its family of numbers, much like the 36B and 77A covered earlier in this book. RM-operated from 31 December 1966, it was already covering the entire Golders Green–Crystal Palace routeing, though differing from the 2 by virtue of operating via Tulse Hill rather than Railton Road and Herne Hill. The route suffered something of a setback in 1972, when it was withdrawn north of Swiss Cottage, but by 1978 had returned to Golders Green. From 4 September 1982 it replaced the 2 entirely north of Baker Street. At the time of its conversion to Routemaster the 2B was shared by Norwood and Stockwell garages, Finchley additionally contributing on Sundays between 1970 and 1978; Victoria was introduced on Saturdays from 1972, Sundays from 1978 and weekdays from 1981. From 25 April of that year Norwood withdrew, its crews spending three years at Clapham while their own garage was rebuilt. That work completed, the Norwood allocation was restored to the 2B on 27 October 1984 in place of both the Victoria and Stockwell shares, the former having already been reduced to weekdays only from 25 June 1983. Even after the showbus era scattered garages managed to keep some RMs in original condition; Norwood's RM47 (VLT 47) looks lovingly cared for in this May 1987 shot; were it not for the modern cars visible in this West Norwood portrait this scene could be mistaken for one from 20 years before. RM47 lasted at Norwood until July 1992 and was then sold, leaving behind its registration. *Geoff Rixon*

Right: Despite the return of Norwood to the 2B on 27 October 1984, Stockwell garage retained an allocation on Saturdays, which, despite being switched to Sundays from 7 February 1987 to see off a short-lived Thornton Heath crew DMS share, finally ceased on 23 May 1987, from which date the 2B was one-manned on Sundays using Norwood's L-class Olympians. Since 21 June 1986 the 2B's service north of Baker Street had been part of new OPO route 82. Further cuts, commencing on 27 February 1988, saw the evening service hived off as OPO route 2A, again with Norwood Ls, and on 10 August 1991 the whole service between Norwood garage and Crystal Palace was allotted to the 2A. The 2B now ran on weekdays only, before 8pm, between Baker Street and Norwood garage, worked by 14 RMLs. This 1989 view of RML2342 (CUV 342C), reposing within its rebuilt home garage, reveals that the 2B had joined a revised network of branded Routemaster routes, marketed under a more discreet 'Bus It!' motif. All that remained, once the parent 2 had been withdrawn late in 1992, was to remove the superfluous 'B' suffix — effected from 27 February 1993. RML2342, although privatised with London General, would move to London United and finish its days in January 2004 on the 94. *Geoff Rixon*

Route 2
Converted from RML to OPO M/OPO L, 29 January 1994

Above: Eleven months after losing its 'B' suffix the 'new' 2 succumbed to OPO. To save the expense of ordering new blinds Norwood's RMLs went around with the 'B' on their number blind painted out in black. The second route 2 required 16 RMLs on weekdays, all coming off by the early evening to allow Norwood's mixed OPO fleet of Ms and Ls to roam the entire route as far as Crystal Palace. Refurbished RML2333 (CUV 333C) shows off its new trafficator stubs and reflective registration plate as it enters Oxford Street from Marble Arch in July 1993. A picture of this bus working from Cricklewood 12 years previously can be seen on page 82, where its subsequent career is also detailed. *Tony Wilson*

Right: The second route 2 restored buses to Marylebone station, a terminus once home to the 1 but abandoned by that route in 1987. At precisely 1.33pm on 26 January 1994, with just two full days to go before OPO conversion, Norwood's RML2653 (NML 653E) has just arrived, with only a dolly stop to greet it. The bus would be transferred to Brixton and spend the next decade there on the 137 and 159, being withdrawn in April 2005 and sold via Ensign to a lucky buyer in Italy. *Richard Moseling*

Route 139
Converted from RM to OPO DML, 28 March 1998

By the early 1990s new Routemaster routes were as rare as hen's teeth, but on 14 March 1992 along came the 139, created to take over the 159's northwest path during a time when routes crossing the capital were being ruthlessly pruned so as to enter Central London from only one direction. The 139 also allowed Chalk Farm garage to sidestep closure one more time. Sixteen RMs were allocated, most transferred from Camberwell, which garage had borne the brunt of losses to the 159 upon its curtailment at Baker Street. Naturally the new 139 was OPO in the evenings and on Sundays, using the Titans then in use from Chalk Farm, and the route, running from Trafalgar Square to West Hampstead, was helpfully projected onward to Golders Green for meal reliefs — something the 159 had not done. Eventually the axe fell on Chalk Farm, the 139 passing to Holloway on 31 July 1993 (and using Ms during the OPO segments). Privatisation of LBL's subsidiaries late in 1994 saw the emergence of MTL London Northern, though the 'Northern' appellation had disappeared when the 139's increasingly dilapidated RM cohort was repainted *en bloc* the following autumn, receiving a darker shade of red not helped by a lack of accompanying white (or cream) relief. RM29 (OYM 453A, ex VLT 29) looks smart as it crosses Oxford Circus in June 1996, but this bus and its fellows couldn't last much longer in their unrefurbished, AEC-engined state; accordingly the 139 was selected for OPO on 28 March 1998, using the latest generation of low-floor Dennis Dart single-deckers. Sold in 1998, RM29 was another bus to make a return to London, joining the 19's fleet in August 2002 and passing on 2 April 2005 to the 159 at Brixton, where it survived until 9 December 2005, the last day of normal Routemaster operation in London. *Geoff Rixon*

Index of Routes